Contents

CONTENTS

About
the author

Lucy Tobin graduated from Lady Margaret Hall, Oxford University with a First in English in 2008. Now aged 23, she is working in London as a journalist for national newspapers including the *Guardian*, *Sunday Times* and *Daily Mail*. This is her first book.

Acknowledgements

To all my friends, thanks for all the fun we had over Alpha Bar lunches, Park End nights, Bod days, 48a mess, laughing, working – and all your help with this book.

Thank you to Anna and Rob for looking after the littlest Tobo; to Howard for the past five years, to G, for being with me all the way!

This book is for my parents, for giving me the opportunity to go to university – and for everything.

Preface

'So, are you excited?' As a soon-to-be-fresher, these were words that I was asked over and over again as I started packing for my new life as a university student. The answer was yes – I was excited to make new friends, to start a new course, to learn to live independently. But I was also pretty nervous. How would I cook for myself every day? What should I pack? Would it be a big jump from A Levels to studying for a degree? Talking to my friends didn't help, since most of them had the same questions – and more.

I arrived at my university halls squashed into the car alongside my mum, dad, and everything I thought I could possibly need. Ever. I didn't quite take the kitchen sink, but I did nick most of the contents of that sink. I thought that my college kitchen wouldn't contain so much as a teaspoon. But as it turned out, it was fully equipped and anyhow my room was so tiny that my parents had to return home with half of my belongings. Plus, I'd still managed to forget some vital items. (Boring though they sound, plug extension cables are really, really useful...)

One drunken night in my third year at uni, some friends and I started compiling a list of all the things we wish we'd known when we started at university. Like the fact that turning up to library induction in freshers' week might actually have been the most useful hour of the whole of the first year. If only we'd done so.

And how to write an essay – it took me three years to discover that one: turns out that adding a couple of extra paragraphs to your AS coursework doesn't really do the job. I realised that academic essays should be written with an entirely different structure. It was eventually cracking that skill that paved the way to my First.

My friends and I didn't stop making new revelations about living independently after freshers' week. And this book isn't just for freshers – the accommodation, work and money tips are useful throughout uni life. In fact, it was during my second year, when I moved into a student house, that I faced a learning curve steeper than the hill I had to walk every day to lectures – and that hill was one of my main forms of student-life exercise.

How to deal with a landlord? How to get your deposit back? How to diplomatically tell our neighbour that his girlfriend's, um, enjoyment noises were just too loud? These were all problems that my housemates and I faced that year. We had to make frequent phone calls home to ask things like, what should we do when the fire alarm wouldn't work? (That was an embarrassing one: the battery had been upside down.) But what we really wanted was someone (or some*thing*: are you getting where this is heading yet?) to answer all our questions.

Then, at my graduation ceremony in September I overheard a fresher telling a friend that she wished that she hadn't bothered buying the whole of the reading list she'd been sent at the beginning of the holiday – it just seemed like a waste of money when all the books were available in the library. Ah, I thought – I remember making that same mistake.

At that moment, I came up with the premise of this guide. Don't expect the usual boring tome of advice that some long-ago graduate cobbled together in an office far from any semblance of uni life. No. This guide is for students, by students (OK, so I've graduated – but until my student card is no longer accepted in Topshop, I'm definitely retaining student status.) My friends and I have already made all the student-life mistakes you could possibly imagine, so you don't have to.

Throughout my time at uni, I also worked as a journalist, specialising on education issues, for papers like the *Guardian* and the *Daily Telegraph*. In my work, I learnt a lot about the big student issues and the inner workings of universities all around the country. That helped me to discover a lot about university life and problems. But what has been most valuable in writing this book has been the daily experiences, whinges, and fun shared by my friends and I during three years at uni. And that's what you'll find in this guide.

Three years will seem like a long time when you arrive at uni, but as I look through the hundreds of photos I've got pinned around my room, I can't believe it's all over. So my most important piece of advice for new students is this: enjoy it. University really is one of the most amazing experiences.

So, are you excited? This book takes care of all the problems – now, you really can be.

Introduction

University starts in freshers' week, and so does this book. The first chapter will steer you through a week when you'll find yourself laughing, crying and drinking more than any other time in your life. There's a handy list of what to pack, plus practical and emotional help to get you through the first few days, and tips on joining clubs and societies. Since everyone's freshers' week is different, you'll also find advice on surviving the week as a non-drinker, plus safety tips on keeping yourself and your stuff protected.

Freshers' week will also be the time when all those moans your parents have made over the past twenty years, about the way that money does not, in fact, grow on trees, will suddenly hit home. At university you'll learn just as much about survival in the real world as you will about academia, so in the second chapter we get down to the business of money. You'll find out how to pick a student bank account (ignore the freebie; a decent overdraft is more useful than a mortarboard-shaped stress ball – really), as well as a bite-size guide to applying for a student loan, having a student job, and paying tax. For those weeks when your wallet feels just a bit too light, there are also loads of imaginative ways to make money, and advice on what to do if you run out of cash.

While we're on the subject of money, you'll also want to work out the way to make it last as long as possible. So Chapter 2 also includes a big chunk on budgeting and controlling your spending, plus loads of websites, money-saving student offers and different ways to help you hoard your cash for more important things... Like chocolate, drink and nights out, obviously.

Accommodation is next up – where to live, who to live with and how to make the most of it will have a huge impact on your day-to-day happiness. Chapter 3 has lots of advice on choosing your accommodation (catered or non-catered, halls or a house?), making the most of your room, and all the practical stuff once you're there. While my student experience involved heading off to live on campus, it's now increasingly popular to stay at home, so you'll also find tips on coping with living at home while studying at uni – all passed on to me by other students who have been there, done that.

If you do opt to live away from home, the first time you feel a sniffle coming on can feel a little scary. Mum's not there with the Lemsip! Dad's not there to write you a sick note! Don't worry – just turn to Chapter 4, where you'll find tips on how to avoid illness and cope with fresher's flu, registering with a doctor and dentist, where to go if you feel ill, first aid, coping with student stress and homesickness, who to talk to if you're feeling down, and info on drink, drugs, sex and smoking. There's also a section on support for students with disabilities.

To help avoid getting ill in the first place, turn to Chapter 5 for food advice. You'll find out information on what to buy, how to go food shopping, learning to cook, and sample lists of what to buy for your store cupboard and fridge. You'll also find student tips on eating and cooking at uni, and hygiene help (if you're scared of killing someone via your cuisine), plus some favourite recipes (for which we need to thank my mum and dad).

Everyone has some advice for university students, especially when they are currently a student or they have just left uni. And when you ask nearly a hundred students about the one thing they wish they had known when they started at uni, you end up with a ton of brilliant advice. So dotted around the book you'll also find loads of tips from students who have been there, done that, and got the beer-soaked T-shirt.

Just when you thought everything was a bit too fun-focused, along came the whole getting a degree thing. At some point you'll have to start attending lectures, writing essays or doing experiments. And it's not easy to jump from the structured school day (or crazy adventures of a gap year) to apparently endless days with a far-off tutorial deadline. So in Chapter 6, you'll find advice on working independently, writing notes, attending lectures, writing a dissertation, tracking down textbooks and citing references – it's all here. And if that wasn't enough packed into one chapter, you'll also discover a bit about studying abroad.

There's also plenty of help for those days that seem so far away but will creep up with surprising speed – exams. Chapter 7 provides advice on coping with exams and revising, uni-style. And despite the fact that we all try our best to choose the right course, accommodation, even university – all these things can turn out to be not as 'right' as they had seemed. So turn to Chapter 8 for a look at the best people to approach if you've changed your mind about one of the big factors in your student life.

Lastly, if I've already foxed you with some kind of slip into uni talk, you'll want to head to the glossary, 'decoding the lingo'. Kinda obvious this one: before I went to uni, I thought a rag was something you cleaned with, but on campus I discovered a whole new meaning. And as for 'matriculation', 'viva' or 'entz', I'd have guessed they were the members of a new indie band before I became a student. So at the back of this book, just before a heap of invaluable sources of further advice from experts in the know, you'll find out what all those strange words mean in studentville.

Chapter 1

Freshers' week

Arriving at uni for the first time, you'll probably feel a bit like you did on your first day at primary school – nervous about the work and teachers (re-branded as tutors this time), excited about meeting new friends, and eager to check out your new surroundings (a whole room this time, and not just a coat peg). You might be a bit keener to say goodbye to the parents this time, and probably won't hang on to their trouser legs as they try to edge towards the door, but don't be surprised if you suddenly feel a tiny bit panicked on the first day. It's natural that you might have mixed feelings when you actually face independence for the first time.

But your first day at uni will be so busy that you won't have much time to stay pondering – you'll be unpacking, organising, learning endless names, forgetting them, getting lost, being found, accepting Facebook friends, swapping numbers, meeting neighbours, eating, drinking and generally rushing around. Freshers' week is a time when you'll smile, laugh, drink, dance, cry and forget hundreds of names. At times you might wish you were somewhere else, at other times you'll wish the week could go on forever. You'll have hours when you love uni, and hours when you hate it – and sometimes you'll feel all these feelings at the same time. That's normal. It's stressful to move to a new place, start a new course, meet hundreds of new people, sift through those people to find friends, arrange a new room, cook and eat new foods, explore a new town, organise new funding, impress new tutors, and go from being top banana in the highest year of school to bottom of the pack as a fresher at university – all within one very busy week.

Arriving at uni: what to expect

When you arrive at university for the first time, with all your stuff, head for your halls of residence or wherever you're living. If you're living in halls, there will probably be a stand set up to welcome you and your family and tell you where to go. If you're living in private accommodation, remember to arrange when and where you will pick up the key before you set off from home.

Once you've arrived in your room (or 'digs', as old people like your parents will probably insist on calling your uni room), it's a good idea to start unpacking as soon as possible. Ask any friends or family who have come with you to help you to unpack before they go, because once your room starts looking nice and homely, you'll feel much happier about settling in.

'I found that freshers' week was an anti-climax – don't worry if you don't enjoy it – uni soon gets better!'
Daniel, 23, Oxford

'Don't expect freshers' week to be the "best week of the year" – it takes time to find your niche and settle down, so freshers' week can end up being more lonely than you might expect.'
Lucy, 21, London

Don't worry about unpacking every little thing (it can be nice to have something left to do when your family leave) but unpack your duvet, make your bed, put up some posters, unload your computer and get out some photos so that your room starts to look like it's your own space.

If you're living in a shared flat or house rather than a single room in a hall of residence, spend a few hours getting to know your new housemates early on. Even if you're more into cleaning than Monica from *Friends*, don't start talking about kitchen cleaning rotas until you've been there for at least a few days – just get to know each other and find things you have in common first. Once you're friends (or at least friendly), sorting out the tough stuff like who's scrubbing the toilet next Wednesday will be easier to organise. (If you're lucky, your hall fee might include the services of a cleaner to do it all for you.)

If you do find yourself feeling homesick, or upset, or stressed, try to relax and then you'll soon start having fun again. One night during my freshers' week, I'd planned to meet a group of coursemates but couldn't remember where we'd arranged to meet – university suddenly felt like a huge place. But the thing about freshers' week is that students and staff will be extra friendly and willing to help out, and give you directions, or dole out advice. So relax, and prepare for a fantastic beginning to your university career. But first you need to pack – so here's a guide to what to put in your case – or, if you're anything like me, your cases…

What to pack

Some things might not apply to you, while other things you might need may not be in the list, but it's a good guide as you start packing for university.

Important documents

- ▶ Accommodation forms
- ▶ Bank account or building society details plus cheque book and bank cards
- ▶ National Insurance card
- ▶ Driving licence
- ▶ Insurance documents including student possessions insurance
- ▶ NHS medical card
- ▶ Your passport or a photocopy of it
- ▶ Plenty of passport photos
- ▶ Documents relating to your student loan

'Take passport photos with you – for some reason you need loads, and if you take them from home at least you don't have to pay...'
Richard, 18, Manchester

Books and academic materials

- ▶ A diary
- ▶ A dictionary
- ▶ You might want some of your old subject notes or books – to be honest, you probably won't use them, but it can be comforting to know that they're there just in case

- ▶ Folders and lined paper
- ▶ Writing paper, envelopes and stamps
- ▶ Pens including highlighters
- ▶ A hole puncher, ruler, scissors, stapler, Sellotape
- ▶ Writing pads
- ▶ A noticeboard (check that your room doesn't already have one first)
- ▶ 'Blu-tack' to stick up posters and room decorations

Toiletries and first aid

- ▶ Any prescription drugs you take
- ▶ Paracetamol
- ▶ Cotton wool
- ▶ Tweezers
- ▶ Condoms
- ▶ Plasters and antiseptic cream
- ▶ A flu remedy to battle against the freshers' flu lurgy
- ▶ All your normal toiletry bag contents – toothbrush and paste, make-up remover, spot cream, etc.

Bedroom things

- ▶ Bedding – duvet, mattress protector, sheet, duvet cover, pillow, pillow covers – but check with your accommodation officer to check what is provided first
- ▶ Hot-water bottle
- ▶ Box of tissues
- ▶ Sleeping bag – for visitors and in case you travel anywhere
- ▶ Laundry bag – to carry dirty clothes to the washing machine (or home...)

'Take dressing-up clothes to uni – there are always loads of dressing-up parties or themed events, so the more crazy hats or wigs or Superman capes you can bring with, the better.'
Lisa, 22, Birmingham

- ▶ Desk lamp (if not provided – check first)
- ▶ Decorative items, e.g. beanbag, cushions, blankets/throws, photos and posters, plants, rug
- ▶ Computer/laptop, plus carry case, charger wires and memory stick
- ▶ Alarm clock
- ▶ Spare batteries
- ▶ Camera
- ▶ Plug extension leads
- ▶ Iron
- ▶ Mobile phone
- ▶ Music player, e.g. iPod

Kitchen goods

Before you start packing your kitchen utensils, check what's provided by your halls or student flat. If your accommodation is

'Take a duvet – I forget mine EVERY term...'
Katie, 18, Aberdeen

> *'Take LOTS of adapters and extension leads for all your knick knacks – hair dryers, straighteners, phone/camera chargers, lamps, kettle, TV, laptop.'*
> Anna, 19, Leeds

self-catered, a lot of the contents listed below will be provided so don't bother wasting your money and save your struggling arm muscles.

- ► Cutlery – usually two or three place-settings of crockery and cuterly is enough, because you can share with friends or housemates, and having loads will just discourage you from washing up
- ► Crockery – plates, bowls, mugs, glasses
- ► Bottle opener
- ► Frying pan
- ► Two saucepans, one small (for the pasta that will probably become your staple diet), one larger (to make soup, etc.)
- ► Chopping board
- ► Sharp knife
- ► Tin opener
- ► Peeler and/or grater
- ► Basic store cupboard foods (e.g. tea, coffee, sugar, cooking oil, herbs, salt, pepper, pasta, rice, cereal, etc.)
- ► Sandwich bags
- ► 'Tupperware' boxes with lids
- ► Cling film, tin foil
- ► Tea towel and oven glove
- ► Cleaning products – like anti-bacterial spray, air freshener, furniture polish if you're really keen – plus dusters. You'll need extra things like toilet and bathroom cleaner if you're living in a

>
> *'I moved to the UK from America for uni, and I was so confused by the "opaqueness" of this place. I mean, I didn't understand that no one in the administration would ever tell you what you needed to know right off the bat – you had to know which questions to ask and who to ask about everything! I found out that the best sources of information (about food, libraries, teaching, admin) were other students – make friends who know what they're doing, or else you're lost! It's all word-of-mouth and sketchy and anxiety-producing, but you soon get into the swing of things.'*
>
> Rachel, 26, studying at Oxford, from California

house. Many halls have weekly cleaners included in your bill, so check first before going to buy Mr Muscle

Extras for international students

► Visas and relevant paperwork

► A copy of your birth certificate and passport

► Travel documents

► Plug adapters for electrical goods

► UK (sterling) currency

► An international phone card

>
>
>
> *'Pack a door stop! I wish I'd had one – our college's rooms all had fire doors that slammed and I wanted a door stop so my room was open for friends to pop in.'*
>
> Adam, 19, Manchester

TIP *'Make sure you meet as many people at you can right at the start, during freshers' week and the winding down time after – some of them may become your best friends, and if you don't get out and about early on, you may never see them again as they get sucked into their workloads and sports commitments and all that.'*
James, 22, Cambridge

The first few days and nights

You'll probably receive a timetable in a freshers' pack when you arrive at your university residence – look after it really well, maybe pin it up on a noticeboard or wall. Make sure you turn up to the first event – probably a big meet-and-greet event in your union or a local café or pub – where you'll be able to meet lots of people in one go. This can seem scary – I remember my parents waving me off, and then what felt like seconds later facing this huge crowd of freshers when I didn't know anyone – but if you plaster a smile on your face, and get chatting to the nearest person, it'll soon seem a lot easier. Remember, everyone's feeling the same as you – even if they look confident, they're probably feeling nervous inside.

There will usually be a big event at the union on the first night. Expect it to be noisy, hot, crowded and overwhelming! And expect a lot of people to drink a lot of booze – but don't worry if you don't want to: more about that later in this chapter. Don't stress if you can't remember the name of half of the people you meet, let alone any of the other stuff you talk about – just swap numbers with anyone you hit it off with, so you can meet up with people later in the week. Swap Facebook details as well as numbers: seeing a photo will help you work out who the hell Rufus Zilner is when he asks to be your 'friend'.

'Get a diary from day one to organise your life.'
Sarah, 18, Kent

Registration

Freshers' week also includes loads of form-filling admin. You'll have to make sure you receive things like student ID and your correct subject timetable as well as to register for your classes. This will probably take absolutely ages and involve massive queues, but think of it as a good chance to make friends as you chat to the people in the queue.

It's best to sort registration out early on, since at many universities you can't collect your loan cheque until you have registered. Once you have done, head to the student finance office to sort out any loans and fees (see Chapter 2, 'Money – getting it and spending less of it'). The finance officers will be experts at the process and will be able to answer any questions. When you receive your loan, bank it as soon as you can – otherwise it can get lost or forgotten until you run out of money, and can't find it.

You should also use freshers' week to register at a doctor and dental surgery (see Chapter 4, 'Health').

Since you'll be so busy, it's a good idea to get a diary before the start of term so you can write down all the events you have to go to, plus all the extra ones you want to go to, and don't miss out on anything. If you need a new one, buy an 'academic year' diary, which starts in September.

'Get the free discount cards from all the shops –
Co-op's Superdividend card, Boots' Advantage
card, Sainsbury's Nectar, Blackwell's reward card,
etc. – they all add up.'
Richard, 22, Manchester

How does freshers' week work?

Freshers' week is the first week of the first term at uni. Most
of your time will usually be filled by events organised by your
Students' Union. You'll be busy doing things like social and
orientation events designed to help you to feel at home on
campus, and will probably receive a freshers' week timetable
at some point during the summer holidays before you arrive
at uni. Events will include things like pub quizzes, library
orientations, tutor meetings, club nights, bowling, ice skating,
and meeting sessions over meals or drinks that offer you the
chance to get together with other people doing your subject.

'I would have appreciated knowing what other
students thought was a normal social life while
at uni – I felt there was too much emphasis on
partying, to the detriment of my studies, and
regret that balance.'
Simon, 25, Manchester

If you're not already a member of Facebook (www.facebook.
com), sign up before you head off to uni, since most students
are members and they use it to organise social events. Some
courses even have academic courses arranged via Facebook
– and by signing up in advance, you might meet people on
your course or in your halls before you head off.

The rest of the week: freshers' fair

The freshers' fair is a huge exhibition of stalls offering everything a student could want, from societies, like sports clubs, music clubs and religious societies, to business services like banks and posters. There'll be tons of freebies too. The fair will usually be held in a huge hall, like the union building or sports centre.

My advice is to turn up at the freshers' fair with a big bag and an open mind – that way, you can fill up the bag with freebies (I scooped a packet of 'Haribo', a bruised apple, loads of cans of drink, three bottle openers, an electronic fan, stationery, key rings and a USB memory stick) while also signing up to groups and societies that might have exciting opportunities to offer you in the future.

There will usually be a list of all the societies offering you membership, probably available on your uni website if not in your freshers' pack. If, after the freshers' fair, you hear of a society that you didn't manage to find, look it up online.

> **TIP**
>
> *'Go for variety when selecting university societies. Choose active and passive activities, things you've done before and things you want to learn how to do. Dance. Play games. Climb walls. Experience politics, cultures and ideas. Learn how to fight, read and sing. Take part in as much as you can. Do not be afraid if you've never done it before and don't be put off by joining fees; the expensive societies usually have the best value for money. Societies are likely to be where you will make your best friends, so choose something that interests you as well.'*
> Curtis, 21, Nottingham

Also most freshers' fairs run for more than one day, so you can usually return to find a group you didn't see earlier (or pick up extra freebies).

While it's true that your prime reason for being at uni is to study, societies, interest groups and sports clubs all offer experiences you might never again come across, plus they will give you the chance to meet new people, have fun and boost your CV. Talk to the students behind the stands about what they do, and if in doubt, sign up – clubs don't usually ask for fees until later on, so you can always drop out later – the only thing to lose is your email storage space...

And it's much better to be really busy in your first few weeks than moping around wondering where everyone else has gone.

I signed up with loads of societies, including student newspapers (after a burst of freshers' week enthusiasm, I never got more involved than reading them), College Choir (forgot to turn up), Rounders Club (did actually do that), Chocolate Appreciation Society (never heard from them again), Photography Society (ended up just snapping away with friends), Tennis Squad (played a few games), Archery (I lasted about as long as the opening credits of *Robin Hood*), Asia Pacific Society (they offered me a free electronic fan – I grabbed it but never became a fan). So while I didn't actually get involved with them all, I was glad that I'd signed up to interesting stuff and had the option of turning up to their events, as I received their emails until the day that I graduated.

Societies, and groups like university newspapers, also offer opportunities to met extra friends away from your coursemates, housemates or fellow halls residents – sometimes you will feel like a break, or might just want to meet up with different people to (whisper it) bitch about your housemates' annoying habits. Societies can offer opportunities to make friends with people that you might not come across in your other social groups.

If you're not a fresher, you haven't missed out – most universities make second, third and older years welcome at the freshers' fair – this might be called something imaginative like the 'refreshers' fair'. So if you always wished you'd joined the bungee jumping club or felt you missed your calling by omitting to sign up at volunteering society, go along to the fair again.

'At Nottingham, the freshers' week nights have a fancy dress theme. I didn't realise you could find out online what the theme was... it would have been useful to know what to bring!' Look on your union's website before setting off to see if any of this kind of info is available.
Sonia, 21, Nottingham

The Students' Union

The Students' Union exists to represent the student body, organise fun events, and help and support in times of trouble. Individual unions will take on slightly different roles, but most will have a big union building, with meeting rooms, a bar and/or café, maybe a shop, sometimes a lounge or games rooms, sports facilities, and offices where students who run the union will work. Usually unions (though note that they are occasionally known as 'guilds') are run by students who have been elected by their fellow students. They normally include a President, supported by a Vice President plus other positions that will vary at each uni but might include a role in charge of Student Welfare, a Woman's Officer, Lesbian/Gay/Bi/

Transgender Officer, Social Secretary, Minority Officer, Mature Students' Officer, International Students' Officer, Campus Co-ordinator, and so on. Some of these roles will be full-time, and involve students taking a sabbatical out of uni work; others are part-time.

If you're interested in taking an active role in helping out with student life, you might want to get involved with the union, but even if not, you should find out where your union is. Students' Unions also arrange a lot of fundraising and charity events such as RAG (Raising and Giving), so ask for more information on this if you're interested – it's another great way to meet people. In fact, you'll find the union to be a good starting point if you have any questions, since the people working there will be able to help you out with issues ranging from problems with accommodation to finding the best place to get in some early food shopping.

What about work?

Don't worry – most universities won't chuck you in at the deep end or expect you to churn out essays in freshers' week – they know that you'll need some time to settle in. That's another reason to make the most of freshers' week opportunities – it might be your only chance to go out and have fun without having to get up early the next day for labs or lectures or having lingering guilt about that essay waiting to be written.

'Take a jumper! You start uni in the month leading up to winter and then it gets cold. Either that, or you'll be complaining that the library air-conditioning is on too high... Those librarians must come from colder climates!'
David, 23, Nottingham

The exception is Oxbridge – they usually do start piling on the work earlier, since their terms are shorter. My official freshers' week at Oxford lasted only a few days, as I had an essay deadline by the Wednesday. Still, your tutors will know that it's still early days and that you will be getting used to using libraries, and adapting to research through lectures and so on at the beginning, so don't worry too much about work during freshers' week, even if you do get given some.

Drinking and going out

During one night out in freshers' week someone told me that school is the place that you learn what alcohol is (in chemistry lessons, not sneaking secret sips of booze from your locker…), and university is the finishing school of 'How To Get Drunk'.

'Get involved with as many extra-curricular activites as possible, then cut down later if you need to. I wish I'd joined stuff I got involved with in my third year much earlier.'
Han, 22, London

Some people worry about how much boozing actually goes on at uni. This doesn't answer the question, but it's a telling tale that a few minutes later, the boozy know-all who had considered himself the star of the drinking 'finishing school' had fallen asleep at the bar, and ended up sleeping through until morning – missing one of the best nights of freshers' week – and waking up with a hangover from hell.

Loads of people worry about how they're going to stay drunk 24/7, as all good students are apparently supposed to, and

'Take lots of box sets of TV shows, films – a good way to make friends is by watching a good comedy or film together, and it's nice, and less lonely in the first few weeks, to have something in the background if you spend a lot of time in your room.'
Danielle, 21, Oxford

graduate with their liver intact – of course, the answer is most people don't drink that much, and quite a few people don't drink at all. You just notice the ones who do because they stand out – they're usually the ones embarrassing themselves by dancing on the table.

Don't let the fact that you're a fresher make you feel under pressure to drink loads. If you weren't a heavy drinker before uni, you don't have to be now – it might seem like everyone is getting drunk, but that's probably because they're hyper with nerves rather than drunk. During freshers' week there are usually always a few people sent to hospital to get their stomach pumped after getting completely off their faces – but they will probably become the subject of heated gossip sessions, miss out on the rest of freshers' week, and for the rest of uni be known as the ones who couldn't have a good time without being drunk. So it's best not to be them.

Another reason to be wary of getting unbelievably drunk during freshers' week is that you may not yet have good friends who you can trust to ensure that you're home safely, or even to remember that you were out with them in the first place. Don't get so drunk that you won't be able to find your way back safely – that way you'll also avoid spending all your freshers' week budget in one night. Remember that alcohol also contains loads of calories, and if you drink loads every night you'll get fat.

In the long term, drinking too much alcohol can have some even worse effects. Some of the illness and diseases associated with alcohol abuse include hepatitis and cirrhosis of the liver, pancreatitis (inflammation of the pancreas), high blood pressure (which can lead to a stroke), gastritis (inflammation of the stomach lining), certain cancers, including mouth and throat cancer, brain damage, heart failure and neurological problems like epilepsy. It can also cause sexual problems like infertility, muscle disease, depression, sleeping difficulties, and skin problems. About two-thirds of suicide attempts are also believed to involve alcohol. So it's not so cool after all.

Drinking advice

No, not a guide to how to unscrew a bottle of vodka, but info on how to avoid getting ill through boozing. First of all, remember that you don't have to drink every time you go out. Try to only drink a maximum of a couple of times a week – you'll probably enjoy the nights off from alcohol and find yourself noticing more and finding out more about your new friends. I'm sure you've heard this before, but maybe you weren't listening – so here goes anyway. Remember to eat dinner before you go out, or failing that have a glass of milk, toast or a banana. Don't go out drinking on an empty stomach, unless your idea of a good night out is one spent with your head dangling on a toilet seat retching.

If you ignore that and do end up drunk, make sure you drink loads of water before you go to bed and when you wake up. You're going to feel bad – this way, you'll feel a tiny bit less bad.

If you have signed up to a club that has initiation rites like drinking games – rugby and other sports squads often have these – take part if you want to, but remember your own limits and don't make yourself ill. If you think that something is being taken too far, don't worry about saying no – in any case, the organisers will probably be too drunk to remember anything in the morning.

If you don't drink at all, don't worry about fitting in. One of my most sociable friends at uni didn't drink – her friends found it a novelty and she didn't let it stop her having a good time. You might want to have a sentence lined up about why you don't drink, since the question might crop up – but make it into a joke if it's not something you want to talk about.

Feeling sad

Being a fresher means that you'll probably have some emotional baggage as well as suitcases full of kettles and cutlery. Anxiety about meeting people and the university social life is not unusual. Like the majority of freshers, in the sixth form years at school my friendship group was well established, and on my gap year I spent most weekends with the same group of friends – so when I started uni I hadn't been meeting new people en masse since the start of secondary school – when we had bonded over issues like how high we could roll up our uniform skirts. After

> **TIP**
>
> 'The whole vaunted university experience doesn't happen immediately. It takes a while to become good friends with someone and I realised that it's quite normal to feel somewhat isolated at university at first. So many friends admitted the same thing after the first few months, but before finding out that other people were having the same experience, I worried that I was doing particularly badly socially.'
> Phil, 22, London

TIP

'Get it into your head from the word go that uni will inevitably have some lows as well as highs. For me they included being mistaken for a toilet and weed on in freshers' week at the Student Union club. And then being told – by my smiling uber-Christian housemate – that I was condemned to hell. Traumatic at the time, but funny when I look back...'
Anon, 23, Edinburgh

having the same reliable, close friends for so long, it's hard not to wish for an immediate new friendship group at university.

According to the National Union of Students (NUS), 50–70% of new UK students suffer from homesickness during their first two or three weeks at uni – so don't worry if you're one of them. If you find yourself feeling lonely in your room at any point, it can be tempting to get out the mobile and call home, or a friend from home. I know, because that's what I did – but it usually makes you feel more homesick.

It's obviously important to keep in touch with home friends and family, and they'll be desperate to hear how you're getting on, but, during freshers' week, rather than spending hours on the phone home, it's a good idea to get out of your room if you're feeling lonely. Head to the union, or common room, or bar, or knock on a neighbour's door – just being around people can help. Once you're surrounded by new people you'll soon be so focused on making conversation with new friends that you'll forget about missing the old ones.

It can be hard, but the best attitude to adopt in freshers' week is to talk to everyone you can – think of it as speed dating for friends: if after a few minutes you're not getting on well with someone, move on – there will be plenty of others around. Remember that everyone arrives at uni looking to make new friends, so they'll be eager to be friendly too.

Above all else, remember to be yourself. The great thing about uni is that anything goes. Every week you'll spot at least a dozen students strolling into lectures wearing outfits that appear to be fancy dress, and there will often be pyjama-clad students pushing their trolleys around Tesco. So if that's the way you've always wanted to do things, make the most of fresher freedom.

If none of these tactics work, and your homesickness or depression is prolonged or feels like it's getting worse, contact your university's counselling or advice centre, which will be able to provide you with support. See more info on homesickness in Chapter 4, 'Health'.

Keeping your stuff secure

In your first year, your room will probably have a lock on the door. Use it, and shut the window, even if you're only going to the shower or kitchen down the corridor – because it's better to be safe than sorry, and also because your stuff is worth more than just cash: in my experience, surviving even a few days of uni without a computer is seriously traumatic. Yeah, it sounds melodramatic – but think about uni life without email, Facebook, YouTube, Jstor and all their online neighbours, and you'll realise that it sucks.

Be sensible about allowing strangers anywhere near your room, too. Don't let people into your accommodation block unless you know them – a policeman once told me that most burglars just follow people in through a door that's held open. Ask for ID if you don't recognise someone, or just let the door slam and they can get out their own key out – or stay out, if they're not supposed to be inside.

Buy a laptop lock – you can get them for about a tenner, and you can use them both in your room (it locks into a USB port, and you loop the other end around something like a table or radiator) and in the library, too – so you can pop to the loo without having to take all your stuff with you.

Take care of your money: use cash machines during the day, not at night, and put your card and cash away quickly. Check that no one snoops at your PIN, and cover PIN machines with your hand to hide your details. Write down all of your card details somewhere safe – including credit cards, ID cards and store cards – so you can cancel them quickly if necessary.

Make a list of the make, model and serial number of all of your electrical items like iPods, laptops and digital cameras, so that if anything is stolen the police can have a crack at tracking down your belongings. It's also important to mark your property with indelible ink, writing down the initials of your university (e.g. MU – Manchester University) and your student ID number. Special security pens might be given away at freshers' week – look out for a local police stall, where I nabbed enough of these special pens to last my whole three years at uni.

Consider taking out student possession insurance from a specialist provider like Endsleigh. If you tot up the value of things you might have at uni, like iPods, laptops, digital camera, mobile, sports equipment, designer clothes, and the rest, you might find your stuff is worth a thousand pounds or more – so it can be worth taking out an insurance policy for a couple of pounds a month. Check with your parents first, because your goods might be covered by their house contents insurance.

Keep yourself safe

Don't make yourself a target for crime – in the day, even if you're loaded with shopping and books, walk confidently and be aware of your surroundings. Don't think of every long walk you have to take as a good time to catch up with friends on your mobile – it's like wearing a neon T-shirt with a built-in megaphone screaming PLEASE ROB ME I'VE GOT VALUABLE GOODS AND I'M SO BUSY CHATTING THAT I'VE GOT NO IDEA WHAT'S GOING ON AROUND ME!!!!!! Stay aware.

It's a good idea to note down your serial number (find out what it is by keying *#06# into your phone), and if your phone is stolen, call your network or 08701 123 123 to immobilise it.

If you're walking around at night, find some other people to go with, walk on the pavement side that faces oncoming traffic, and buy a safety alarm – check out your union shop, or ask your welfare officer as they're often available for discounts or even free. Keep it somewhere where it's easy to grab if you need it. Alternatively, go by bike or cab if you're alone and it's isolated.

When you're about to get onto a bus or train, have your ticket or cash ready in your hand or loose in your pocket so you don't have to show off your wallet to potential burglars. Try to find somewhere that's bright and well lit and near other people while you wait.

Once you get on board a bus or train, sit near the driver, especially if there aren't a lot of people around. And always have the number of a registered taxi company on your mobile – ask your union or freshers' week representative for a reputable company, and put a copy in your wallet too, since, in my experience phones always run out of battery at the worst time. When you book a cab, ask for the driver's name, and the type of car, so you can check out the details when the car turns up. And definitely don't take up the offer of a 'cab' from those dodgy guys that hang out outside clubs at chucking-out time.

If you're out drinking, make sure that your drinks don't get tampered with – watch your glass or bottle, and hold on to it too. If you do find that your drink smells or tastes weird, don't keep sipping it to make sure – just put it down, stop drinking, and ask a friend to check that you're OK during the rest of the evening, and to accompany you home. Since some date rape drugs can't be seen or tasted, tell a friend or someone working in the bar if you feel at all ill, woozy or light-headed and seek medical advice. For more student safety tips see www. suzylamplugh.org/tips.

Some do's and don'ts about freshers' week

▶ Do sort out your finances as soon as possible – see Chapter 2 on money.

▶ Don't feel like it's the end of the world if you don't join in with absolutely everything – I ended up watching films and doing crosswords with a girl I hadn't met before on one night in freshers' week – we'd both needed a night off from meeting people, and ended up becoming best friends.

▶ Do download an internet telephone service like Skype to keep in contact with both new and old friends for free on your computer.

▶ Don't accept your accommodation if you're unhappy. The accommodation office will expect that not all the groupings they arrange will be successful. If someone is making your life difficult,

> 'Communication is really important. Join Facebook, and get a good contract for your mobile before you arrive at university, so you can stay in contact with everyone easily. If you go to study abroad, spend money on a local mobile contract.'
> James, 20, Nottingham

or something is physically wrong with your accommodation, speak to the housing officer – sooner rather than later.

▶ Do join societies that match your interests – or inspire new ones. I met new people doing things as diverse as archery, badminton, and on the committee of a garden party.

▶ Do keep in contact with home – your parents will want to know you're OK, and it can make you feel better to know that someone you love is looking out for you from afar.

▶ Don't panic if you think you don't fit in – it's early days and you're bound to make friends soon.

▶ Don't pull too many people too early on – it's harder to lose a bad reputation than it is to make one.

▶ Do register with a local doctor and dentist – see Chapter 4.

▶ Do have a map of campus and the local town for those inevitable times when you get lost.

▶ Do swap mobile numbers early on – even if the people you're swapping numbers with aren't going to be your best buddies, it's a good idea to have the number of someone nearby who you can meet up with in the first few days.

▶ Do attend all the meetings that have been scheduled by your university or freshers' week organisers, since they will probably be where you sign up for modules, receive passwords and organise your timetable, and it will take much longer to organise all of that stuff on your own.

▶ Don't forget your old friends – after a month or so, when you're settled in, invite them to stay with you for a weekend and introduce them to your new mates.

▶ Do attend library tours and induction meetings. I didn't, and spent the rest of my three years gazing blankly at the shelves hoping that I'd somehow understand a seemingly impenetrable classification system, and wishing I'd attended that induction meeting. If you do miss it, ask the librarian early on for a catch-up session.

Chapter 2

Money

The cost of uni is a massive issue for most students, so it's important to sort out exactly how much you're going to have to pay, and exactly how much money you're going to be able to borrow or earn, before you start taking your seat at lectures. That way, while you're in these lectures, instead of worrying about your empty wallet, you'll be able to focus on studying postmodern transcendentalism or nuclear fusion ... or just concentrate on feeling guilty about missing said lectures while studying the local bar's drinks menu.

Loads of ways to get your hands on cash

And none of them are illegal. First things first: make sure you're fully aware of any loans or grants that you're eligible for – and know the difference between a loan and a grant. Loans have to be paid back. Grants don't. But while everyone will be eligible for a loan of some amount, grants are available only to certain students, usually limited by factors like family income.

If possible, sort out all of the below financial issues way before freshers' week, preferably in the summer holidays, when you'll find people like student finance officers are much less busy and easier to contact. That way, you have enough money at uni from the very first day when you reach into your pocket to finance the first bar crawl.

The cost of study: tuition fees

Maximum annual tuition fees for students in England, Northern Ireland and Wales starting a course in 2009 are £3,225. The amount you will have to pay will depend on your household income – that's the total earnings of your parents or guardians. There's more detail below, but note that the tuition fee information is different for students in England, Northern Ireland, Wales, and Scotland: see the separate sections on each nation.

Tuition fees in England

These are £3,225, but do not have to be paid upfront. You can pay when you have graduated and are earning more than £15,000. See below, 'Paying for tuition: the student loan'.

Tuition fees in Northern Ireland

As in England.

Tuition fees in Wales

Welsh universities also charge top-up fees of up to £3,225, but students living in Wales only have to pay £1,285. Students from England, Scotland and Northern Ireland studying in

Wales will have to pay the full fees if they go to university in Wales. Likewise, if Welsh students choose to study in England, Northern Ireland or Scotland, they have to pay the full fees of that nation.

Tuition fees in Scotland

Scottish students studying at Scottish universities do not have to pay fees. Students from England, Wales and Northern Ireland studying in Scotland will have to pay the full fees if they go to university in Scotland, but these are lower than elsewhere in the UK. Standard degrees cost £1,775, while medicine degrees cost £2,825. Scottish students who choose to study in England, Wales or Northern Ireland have to pay the full fees of £3,225.

Paying for tuition: the student loan

If you have been living in the UK for at least three years before the start of your course, you'll be able to take out a student loan to cover the full cost of tuition fees, which is up to £3,225.

Since this loan is not means-tested (so the government give it to all students, regardless of their income or their parents'

'Check what's included in your rent. I lived in halls and thought everything was included, but I got billed – a lot – for staying a couple of extra nights at the end of term.'
Shaun, 23, Birmingham

income), nearly everyone is eligible. But there are a few exceptions – just to keep your brain ticking over. For example, people who have previously been through uni cannot usually receive this loan. But for the majority of readers, this loan will be available. It is paid directly to your university.

In the same blitz of form filling you'll be asked if you want to take out a loan of up to £6,928, to cover the cost of living. This loan – sometimes called a 'maintenance loan' by people in suits – is paid directly into your bank account, and split into three equal instalments throughout the year. You'll be able to spend it on whatever you want – but it's best to stick to things like accommodation, food, drink, etc., rather than buying a small island off the coast of New Zealand.

All students can receive 75% of the maximum maintenance loan, but receiving the extra 25% depends on things like where you are studying (London university students can receive more) and your household income – that will usually mean your parents' earnings. It can also be impacted by your relationship status – not how many times you've dumped and got back together with your boy/girlfriend, but whether you're married or not. Married students are classed as 'independent students', meaning finance support is calculated according to personal circumstances, not parental income. That's also true if you're over 25, or have a baby, or are an orphan, or have been financially supporting yourself for at least three years.

If you don't need your loan money immediately, don't leave it in your student account – invest it to earn more interest. Georgia, a student at Nottingham, was very financially savvy. 'I opted to invest my student loan into an unlimited-access Individual Saving Account [also known as an ISA] at the beginning of each year, and that way it was earning money while my student account was still in the black, and then, towards the end of term when I was about to run out of money, I withdrew the cash from my ISA.'

When to apply for funding

You can apply for loans any time after March of the year that you're heading to university. It's best to apply as soon as you can, to ensure the cash comes through to you on time. However, you can still apply up to nine months after the first day of your academic year – that usually means up to May in the year following the time you started uni.

Be aware that even if you are flush enough to opt not to have a student loan (and even if you really, really hate to fill in forms), you still have to apply for the tuition fee funding, because otherwise you will end up paying full whack on course fees. You might not realise it, but university actually costs a lot more than the £3,225 maximum tuition fee limit – your education is subsidised by the government. That's why tuition fees are often called 'top up' fees.

So you do need to apply for the tuition fee funding to ensure that you don't end up having to pay full whack.

If you do opt to take out a loan to cover tuition fees, you might want to know that you don't actually pay these loans back until you have a job that includes a salary of more than £15,000 a year. So now can you see why those five minutes of form filling are more important than *EastEnders*? Or even A Level revision, frankly.

How to apply for funding

Confusingly, this depends on where you live. There are two options: you will either have to contact the Student Loan Company (SLC – www.slc.co.uk) or your Local Education Authority (LEA). Some boroughs use the SLC to sort out their local students' loans, others do it themselves. To find out which to contact in your area, start off at the government's explaining website: www.direct.gov.uk/studentfinance. There is an MSN-style chat provider on the site, so you can ask any questions.

Another source of advice is the finance officer at your uni – they all have one – and they'll know the process back to front. Mine offered personalised advice and would always email me back immediately.

Paying for university: the Maintenance Grant

Some students from England who are doing full-time uni courses are also eligible for Maintenance Grants – that's cash that you don't have to pay back, which you'll be able to apply for through the main student finance application. It's worth up to £2906 a year.

These grants are available to students whose household income is less than £50,000. They're means tested, so the maximum cash is only available if your household income (that's the combined income of your parents or guardians) is below £25,000 a year – if that's the case for you, you'll be eligible for a Maintenance Grant of £2,906. There are also smaller amounts available to students whose household income is higher, up to

'I wish I'd known about average living costs, especially utility bills. The inhabitants of my flat were overcharged at one point during my second year at uni, and it wasn't until I showed my dad the bill that he told me electricity couldn't be that expensive. So compare costs before paying bills.'
Kaajal, 22, Nottingham

that £50,000 limit when the government decide your family is rich enough to pay for you themselves…

In Wales, the Maintenance Grant is called the 'Assembly Learning Grant' and is up to £2,906 (for 2009/10) support for eligible Welsh students. The actual amount depends on household income and will be worked out by your local authority.

Another type of grant – the Special Support Grant – is also available: this is money of the same value increments, but offered to students who are single parents or have certain disabilities. For more information on both these types of grant, contact your local authority. You'll find their contact details on the same government site – www.direct.gov.uk/studentfinance for English students, www.studentfinanceni.co.uk for Northern Irish students, www.studentfinancewales.co.uk for Welsh students and www.saas.gov.uk for Scottish students.

Tracking down bursaries

Bursaries are sums of money that you do not have to pay back. They are organised and offered by universities and by other organisations such as educational trusts and charities.

Most are restricted to students whose families have low incomes, for example students who are paying the maximum tuition fees (£3,225) and are receiving the maximum Maintenance Grant (£2,906) will be eligible to receive a bursary from their university. This is about £319 for the year, but can be a lot more – so ask your uni.

It is definitely worth spending an hour or so online to see if you can find anything you're eligible for. Be imaginative:

think about things like possible charity funds (e.g. some local churches might have money available for church members who go to uni), career-related money (e.g. NHS bursaries are available for some medical courses – see www.nhsstudentgrants. co.uk) and alumni groups (some keeno ex-students like to give money for other students to do the same course as them, so find out if there is any alumni cash available from your old school or new uni). A good place to start is this site: http:// bursarymap.direct.gov.uk, which has a map providing direct links to universities' own bursary information pages.

Getting sponsored

Some flush companies pay students cash while they're studying, usually on the basis that the student will work in that company for a set amount of time after graduation. Most students in this lucky position have made these links during gap years. One of my uni friends worked at the big accountancy firm PriceWaterhouseCoopers during her gap year, and they then paid her a set amount of money each year that she was at uni, plus extra cash to work for them over summer, in the hope that she'd sign up as their employee after graduating. Nice work if you can get it.

Another common way of getting uni sponsorship is through the armed forces (see www.armyjobs.mod.uk/education/ grants/Pages/FurtherEducationBursary.aspx). The army scheme, for example, offers £1,000 a year to recruits who sign up to the army and study courses in certain areas, such as IT, engineering, catering and languages. Recruits receive a further £1,000 when they complete military training.

To find out more about other kinds of sponsoring companies, contact your uni careers officer, who will usually be happy to chat about it even before you actually start term – just phone up the careers service.

Finding scholarships

If you achieved especially good A Levels (or equivalent qualifications), or if you get good results while at uni, you might be able to find scholarship funds that will give out money as a 'congratulations' prize. Check with your university and old school, as these depend on things like subjects, results, etc. A few of my friends at various unis won bursaries after amazing first-year exam results.

TIP

'Look for arthouse cinemas in your local city – better films, cheaper prices.'
Henry, 19, Bristol

Making friends with the bank: getting an overdraft

Newspapers, friends, family – they will all tell you to choose a student bank account based on its overdraft rather than its freebie. And I know sometimes piggy bank-shaped stress balls can be really, really desirable. And I know that practical-sounding freebies can be an ever bigger draw – for ages, NatWest has been offering a free 16–25 railpass, offering proper discounts on rail travel.

If you're not going to need an overdraft, fine – make the most of the rail discount, or free MP3 player, or stuffed pig, or

'Try to organise your student bank account before you get to uni – it will save you loads of time standing in a queue!'
AJ, 25, Oxford

whatever. But if you know you're going to be at risk of running short of cash, the size of the interest-free overdraft should be the most important thing you compare when looking at student accounts.

But even though I knew all of that, I still ended up asking my dad what an overdraft actually was. Now I've learnt all about them, here are the facts. An overdraft is the 'minus money' in your account. So if you only have £20 in your bank account and go and buy a Topshop coat for £80, you'll be £60 overdrawn. If you have an account without an overdraft facility, the bank will charge you money for 'borrowing' that £60 from them. But if you do (and many student accounts will let you have overdrafts of £1,000+, with the overdraft amount usually growing every year that you're at uni), then you won't have to pay a penny for borrowing that cash. But it's only a 'free' overdraft if you pay back the money before the time limit comes in.

Some important things to remember if you do opt to have an overdraft: don't go 'above' the overdraft – that is, don't borrow more than the amount the bank has said is your limit. If you do, they'll start charging you hefty overdraft fees. My flatmate once arranged to pay our whole house's electricity bill from her account. But she forgot to ask us for the money before the electricity people took the money from her account. Cue a big penalty and a spate of crying, followed by a week eating supermarket own-brand cereal for every meal.

If you do think you're going to need to borrow more money than your overdraft allows you to, speak to the bank first. If you speak to Mr or Mrs Bank Manager (or, more likely, their call centre representative from Mumbai) a decent amount of time before you hit the limit, they're more likely to be generous and let you have more flexibility about borrowing from them.

It's also worth phoning the bank if you go over the overdraft – especially if it's only a few pennies or pounds over: you'll be hit with a penalty automatically by the bank's computers (computer says no, if you like), but if you call up to explain that you didn't realise your wages hadn't gone through yet, or some other likely excuse, that might result in the bank waiving the fees.

But that's only likely to work once. So it's best to just say no to that £100 cashmere jumper, and you don't need the latest mobile phone. And that pricey DVD-buying addiction can probably be curbed too. But for those spending sprees that you really can't resist, see below for some more imaginative money-earning ideas.

How to do banking

I've just remembered the boring hours I spent queuing in the bank and waiting to speak to a call centre before I discovered online banking. There will be loads of different banking transactions to sort out while at uni, from rent to utility bills and your mobile bill, and setting up an online account means you can check your balance, see if anyone's been helping themselves to your money, send money over to other people and companies, all at the touch of a button. Well, actually you'll have touched 52 buttons after you've filled in all the passwords and security gizmos, but still, better than queuing up at the bank. You can also check if you're approaching your overdraft limit.

Whisper it... you could get a job...

75% of UK students have some kind of job while at uni. Whether you get a job during the holidays or during term time, there are lots of benefits – the wage is an amazing income boost, there are possible freebies, it's a nice break from the student bubble, and it's good for your CV.

But make sure the hours don't dramatically impact your uni life as you'll probably only be there once. Remember you'll probably be working for the rest of your life, but sitting around drinking coffee as you debate how to fix the world in the Students' Union – that's a once-in-a-lifetime opportunity!

Be aware that most unis recommend that students don't work more than 10–15 hours per week. If you can get it, casual work can be the perfect way to fit in work and uni, and if you have any special skills to offer, the money can be better than bar work too.

Finding work

See if your campus has a job shop – this is a student employment agency, which works like a normal job agency but usually won't take a commission. Or try to sell any skills that you're particularly expert at. I worked as a freelance journalist for newspapers throughout my university career, often writing about student issues that other journalists, stuck in their London offices, didn't get to hear about. A photographic friend worked by taking pictures at weddings on some weekends, a musical friend used to play the piano at people's parties or uni balls.

People will pay money for surprising things – so make the most of your talents! If you're strong, you might be able to do some work helping people move house. If you're good at computers, you could teach IT to people in your uni neighbourhood. Some good places to advertise or look for work include local halls and churches, the Students' Union, the local newspaper, plus websites like www.gumtree.com or www.studentgems. com, a specialist site for students to advertise skills for other people (or businesses) to pay for.

Holiday work

You might be able to make more cash working intensively in the holidays, saving up for the term time, than working now and then during the term. Some big companies, mainly banks and law firms, offer lucrative salaries for students on summer internships, which are generally targeted to students at the end of their second year.

The financial rewards can be huge – sometimes up to £10,000 for a summer's work – but for such big sums you should be ready to say goodbye to your social life: a few of my friends spent a summer working crazy hours, from 7am until 2 or 3 in the morning. I think they call it selling your soul… And I stayed away. But if you fancy caviar for lunch in the third year, one of these internships might be worth considering.

Tax

Your first scarily addressed letter with the 'Revenue and Customs' logo on the envelope is a memorable piece of post. It can be annoying to give away your hard-earned cash to the taxman. But since we have to, it's best to do it the right way from the start, to avoid paying too much. So here are the facts.

▶ Most students who work are classified as 'employees' – you work for someone else, who sorts out the tax for you. Easy.

▶ You're allowed to earn a certain amount of money every year that is not subject to income tax: between 2009 and 2010 it's £6,035. If you earn any more than that in a year (the 'year' is classified as 6 April–5 April), you have to pay tax on the extra amount. That's called income tax.

▶ The percentage of tax you have to pay gets bigger as your earnings grow. The more you earn, the more tax you pay.

If you're earning more than £6,035 and paying income tax, you also need to tell your bank, who will deduct tax from any savings you've got mounting up in there. (By now you may be thinking that it's better to spend it on beer, but shove it in the bank and you'll be able to afford some champagne when you graduate.)

You might also be going off the whole getting a job idea by now, but if not bear with me; there's more tax to be paid. You'll also have to pay National Insurance, which, one day in your grey-haired future, will go towards your state pension and other such goodies. Your employer will deduct this from your wages too. Find out exact amounts and get more help at www.hrmc. gov.uk/students.

If you're just working a little bit, for example, you work for a few weeks over the Christmas holidays, and don't think you'll earn more than £6,035 a year, tell your employer that you're a student and that you need to fill in form P38(S). That way you won't pay tax from your earnings and it will save you lots of time in the long term. If you forget to do this, and find that your wage slip has had tax deducted but you haven't earned more than £6,035, ask for a form P50. This will result in the taxman giving you a refund.

If you have a job where you're not an employee, for example you work on a freelance basis doing one of the things mentioned above, like IT help, and you earn more than £6,035, you'll have to register yourself as self employed and pay tax to the taxman by yourself. See www.hmrc.gov.uk/selfemployed for more details.

Earning money in other ways

Here is a quick-fire list of ways that my friends and I have earned money from during university, some reluctantly provided by a friend whose forte was earning money while staying in bed (she worked on her laptop from bed…).

▶ Become a mystery shopper. Google 'mystery shopping' or sign up at www.retaileyes.co.uk to earn money for visits to restaurants, clubs, hotels, gyms, shops. The earnings aren't great, usually about £10 per visit, but if you were going out to the shop/restaurant anyway, you'll make savings too. I got three months' free gym membership as a mystery shopper. And a free eyebrow wax. I'm not sure which was more painful.

▶ Speak to your Students' Union, university admissions office and faculty office about ways to earn money. Some unis pay students to take tours, do admin, work in bars, etc. We were given free lunches if we spent the lunch chatting to wannabe students about uni life. Some friends reported that their lunch 'dates' were really hot. So yeah, there is such a thing as a free lunch. If you've got this kind of job, your employer will probably be more sympathetic to excuses like 'I can't work today, I have an essay crisis' than normal employers.

▶ Blog your way to riches: if you write a popular blog with lots of readers, you can make money through ads. See, for example, www.google.com/adsense. A less ethical option is sponsored blogging: sites like www.payperpost.com let companies pay you to praise their products in a blog. Does that count as taking from the rich to feed the (student) poor?

▶ Sign up with online survey or market research sites. Some local groups will run meetings for you to attend – I once earned £30 for reading a new medicine's instruction leaflet and then answering the easiest questions I'd ever heard. Things like 'Is this medicine an "adult pill" or "suitable for children to eat like sweets?"' Easy money, I say. Also sign up for online research groups like www.yougov.com – the money is much less, about £1 a survey, but it all adds up and you can do it from bed. See – there's nothing dodgy about working from bed in studentville.

▶ Become a campus brand manager. Companies as varied as Apple (the computer firm, not the fruit), Nike and big banks and law firms hire students to boost their campus credentials. Find out more by looking online. Some pay via commission, others on a termly basis, while others provide company freebies.

What to do if you run out of cash

If you run out of money while at university, maybe because your student loan has not come through yet, your university might be able to offer you the chance to dip into their 'Access to Learning Funds'. These are provided by universities to help you out with things like emergency payments to cover financial crises or just aspects of everyday living that you can't afford for some unforeseen reason. They are available for students in serious financial problems, including those considering quitting uni because of financial difficulties, students with childcare costs and disabled students.

Some of these 'Access to Learning Funds' will be (non-repayable) grants, others will be loans – this depends on each individual university and each student's circumstances. If you hit serious money problems, or are struggling with money in any way, try to contact university advisors as soon as possible: they will tell you about options that may help.

How to spend less money

Uni is traditionally known as a time for poverty. But it doesn't have to be. There are lots of ways to boost your earnings (and cut your spending) while still having a good time. For example, after my three years as a student I now find it nearly impossible to go out for a meal at a restaurant without a buy-one-get-one-free offer.

'Write down how much you spend for the first month – that way you can work out what you're spending on necessities and what's being wasted on extras.'
Sam, 20, London

Every time I had a lunch or dinner out, I looked online first to find restaurants running vouchers, print one off, and enjoy my meal for half-price. There are downsides: I've eaten more portions of Wagamama's chicken ramen than anyone should do, but it meant a hot meal, it was next door to the library, and after splitting the bill with a friend the whole thing cost £3! Here's how to maximise earnings and cut costs while living in studentville.

Make a budget

Budgets help to prevent the last few weeks of term being really boring: eating toast, and not going out, because you have no money is rarely very fun.

'Before term, I go shopping in my kitchen at home – as in, my family home. Just get a big bag, go through the cupboards, and put anything that looks tasty or useful into your bag. It's much cheaper than the supermarket!'
Al, 22, Birmingham

I waited until a few weeks into uni before realising that actually it would be a good idea to work out how much I was spending – that was bad planning. Since freshers' week will probably be one of the most expensive weeks you'll encounter at uni, try to work out a budget before you arrive to avoid spending a week's cash on one night out.

Student expenses vary wildly – some of my friends living at home, just walking distance away from campus, could get away with spending only about £2,000 a year (I'm not including tuition fees in this calculation, since you don't have to pay for them until after graduation – unless you're particularly keen to do so, in which case a strict budget isn't an issue).

But other friends, living away from home, renting accommodation, buying food, drink, books, plus shelling out for travelling costs, spent more like £10,000 a year. London-based students used to whinge most about prices. In big cities it's not only accommodation that costs more, but also drinks, food, clothes – pretty much everything, really.

So here's the lowdown on making a budget. Get a big blank piece of paper (or do it on a computer spreadsheet, if you're that way inclined). Make a list of all your incoming cash for the year. Everyone's budget will be unique but here are things you might be able to include on yours: loan, savings, funds from the bank of mum and dad (plus grandparents, aunties, fourth cousins twice removed, teddy bears, etc.), term-time work, holiday work, any grants, bursaries, scholarships and so on.

You might need to put your amount of bank overdraft in here too, but, if possible, leave this out for use in case of unforeseen purchases, like the end-of-year balls and parties (and outfits to wear at them, obviously…).

Next on to the page should be a list of expenses that you expect to have to shell out for over a whole year. Things to consider including are: rent, utility bills, food, going out and entertainment costs, travel, course costs like field trips and textbooks, printer cartridges, stationery, mobile bills, clothes, emergency money, insurance, car-running costs, bike-running costs, any holiday funds, cigarettes, medical costs (including things like contact lenses), presents. This list isn't exhaustive. To make your budget as accurate as possible, go through your bank account or wallet to remind yourself of the kinds of things you regularly buy. And add them all to your long list of expenses.

Next, add a lump sum to spend on freshers' week – it might seem extravagant to flash the cash in your first week of a probably poverty-filled three years, but think of it as expenses – having fun and making friends will make you happier; if you're happier you'll work better and get a higher degree; if you get a high degree you'll get a better job and earn more. Simple maths. The cost of my freshers' week fun was about £300. I know that sounds loads, but I spent about £100 of that joining various clubs and societies, which saves money in the long run.

So now you've got two lists, it's time to add some numbers. Some figures you will know already, like rent if you've already chosen a flat or room, but others you'll have to estimate – like the cost of going out during the year. Here are some average figures to help you with your budget, but remember they will vary depending on a huge range of factors from your university's location to the kinds of food you like to eat.

- ▶ Average cost of rent per week – UK average: £62, London: £102*
- ▶ Average cost of utility and phone bills per week – £23.35†
- ▶ Average cost of supermarket food per week – £21.48†
- ▶ Average cost of going out per week – £15.97†

*figures from Accommodationforstudents.com research
†figures from NatWest 2008 survey.

Add up these costs or your own approximations, plus all those that you know for certain, then take away any non-essential living costs, like going out, car expenses, etc. Here you have a rough figure of the money you'll need to survive a year at uni. Let's call it 'x', since I haven't used that phrase since year 10 algebra, and it makes us all feel clever.

Then add up the total funds you're going to have – the first column – and deduct that figure 'x'. We're nearly there now: the last step is for you to divide the remaining amount of cash between all the non-essential things you listed. You might want to consider putting these in order of preference, so if you're obsessed with not wearing glasses, then spending money on contact lenses will be more important to you than, say, running a car.

I was always rubbish at maths, so here is that budgeting formula again:

First work out total available funds, then minus the cost of essentials. Then split the remaining cash among your other outlay.

For example, if a total termly budget was £800, the following budget would work. The student has allowed more spending at the beginning, when he or she is spending more on books, going out and buying staples at the supermarket.

Week number	Food (super-market and eating out)	Going out	Bills	Extras (photo-copying, books, clothes, DVDs, etc.)	Travel	Total
One	£26	£20	£15	£20	£20	£101
Two	£30	£32	£9	£21	£18	£110
Three	£18	£19	£15	£11	£15	£78
Four	£20	£12	£19	£32	£20	£103
Five	£27	£9	£25	£21	£16	£98
Six	£20	£22	£19	£12	£18	£91
Seven	£19	£29	£5	£9	£25	£77
Eight	£17	£16	£21	£12	£15	£81

To really break it down, you could then divide the amounts by the number of weeks you're at uni, to help you to work out how much you should be spending every week. Once you start uni, your priorities might change or estimations differ, so it's a good idea to write down all your spending and earnings for the first few weeks – that way, your next budgeting session will be more accurate – don't stick to one for your whole uni career.

There is a more high-tech version. You'll still need to work out all of your earnings and outgoings and spending, but if you use the website www.studentcalculator.org.uk, the site's formulae will work out your budget for you. It's backed by personal finance company UniAid plus the NUS, government and banks. If you set up a free account with the site, you'll be able to save and adapt the budget throughout your time at uni.

The whole shebang will help to keep you solvent throughout uni, and for arts students like me there is an extra benefit:

the chance to use a bit of the old GCSE Maths skills to stop your adding and subtracting disappearing to the place that trigonometry ran off to a long time ago. Brushing up on skills and saving money – it's kind of like a buy-one-get-one-free offer – and they're next on the agenda anyway.

Save money on travel

Travel is one of those things that's annoying to splash out on – you don't have any tangible benefits at the end, apart from maybe a ticket stub, or some less-tired legs so save money on it. First of all, don't take a car unless you need one. Most uni campuses are easy to walk around, and will have public transport for all the main routes to halls, the supermarket, etc., since so many students will be making these journeys. There are often student discount cards available for local bus or train journeys – ask older students or speak to someone at your Students' Union. For longer, national journeys, check whether it's worth buying a 16–25 railcard, which will give you about a third off the full price of a ticket, but costs around £26 a year.

If time is not that important, take the coach rather than the train – it's normally cheaper, but shop around when booking to check. Whatever you choose, try to book in advance to nab a cheaper ticket. Look at all the options that will take you to your destination – Megabus, for example, offers discounted coach journeys; National Express coach journeys are also normally cheaper than train tickets. You can buy a student

'Pack a pair of comfortable shoes – you'll end up doing lots of walking on campus.'
Jon, 19, Birmingham

TIP

'Look up car sharing on uni noticeboards. It's great if you're not living on campus – I'm at Bath uni; instead of paying £8 a week on the bus, I now spend £3 a week in petrol contributions to a fellow student. I save about £120, and it keeps me from waiting in long bus queues.'
James, 20, Bath

coach discount pass too. In London, buses are cheaper than the Tube, and if you're a student at a lot of unis you'll also be eligible for a free student Oyster card, giving you discounted Tube travel cards, so ask your local Tube station for an application form.

Walk or cycle where possible. It's cheap and healthy. and if you have to take cabs, share the ride with a friend – that makes it cheaper and safer. If you do think that you will need a car (and I have to be honest here – I took mine even though I could have lived without it), then find ways to save money. Offer people lifts and ask them to give you petrol money – if it saves them the bus fare and means a door-to-door ride, they won't mind and they'll understand that you need to cover your costs. That's especially true if you're going on a longer journey – taking a trip home, for example, you should ask around first if anyone needs a lift to a similar kind of area – they'll appreciate the lift and you can easily ask for £5 or £10 towards the journey, depending on the distance, of course.

Other imaginative ways to save money

▶ You'll know that you're a real student when your heart rate speeds up when you hear the word 'freebie'. If a big company is advertising on your campus, they'll often be offering to take students out for meals to talk about their graduate jobs. And so

> *'It's way cheaper if you buy toiletries in bulk – a big bottle of "Tresemme" shampoo is better than a tiny expensive bottle of "Aussie"!'*
> Cherie, 22, Staffordshire

long as you focus on your food when the spiel starts, you'll be enjoying a truly free lunch.

▶ Use your student discount card wherever possible.

▶ If you're having to pay extra for electricity bills, charge up things like your mobile and laptop when you're on campus – like in the library. Every penny counts!

▶ If you're buying anything over £5, check online whether you can find a discount coupon first. They're available from a huge range of shops, from clothes stores to photo developing companies, so it's worth a few minutes searching to save money. Check out, for example, www.vouchercodes.co.uk, www.myvouchercodes.co.uk and www.moneysavingexpert.com. Or use a search engine like Google to search the name of the shop you're buying from and 'discount' or 'coupon'.

▶ Use buy-one-get-one-free coupons when going out for a meal – and search in advance so you can choose a restaurant based on a cheap deal.

▶ Cook using fresh food and vegetables rather than ready meals – see Chapter 5 for more details.

▶ Save money on utility bills by limiting the time you have the heating on, taking showers not baths, and sending emails rather than phoning.

▶ Go to bars that are marketed for students – they'll normally be cheaper.

▶ Find free entertainment – for example free tickets to TV shows (see websites like www.applausestore.com and www.bbc.co.uk/tickets).

▶ Go to student theatre and music productions – some are really good. (OK, so you'll probably find yourself dragged along to these by a friend who was the star of the show, but it can still be a fun and cheap night out.)

▶ Don't buy books or DVDs unless you really have to, for example you need to write notes in a course book or need a book really often. Instead, borrow from friends, libraries and faculties. If you do need to buy a book, check out second-hand bookshops. For course books, ask a recent graduate if you can buy his or her old ones off them. See Chapter 6 for more details.

▶ Go to the supermarket at the end of the day so you can take advantage of reduced foods. See Chapter 5.

▶ Don't pay full whack for a haircut – look for local hairdressers offering modelling sessions, when you can get a haircut for a tenner or less. Or, if you're really brave, ask a friend to get involved with some clippers. Mmm, nice mullet.

▶ Meet up at a friend's house to eat and drink before a night out so you save money on booze.

Chapter 3

Halls and housing

Choosing the ideal accommodation for your needs (and finances) while you're at uni is a really important decision, especially in the first year – since the roof over your head can affect loads of issues, not just the luxury of your surroundings, but things like security, food, how much spare cash you'll have and the number of new people you meet. This chapter looks at the kinds of accommodation options you'll have – university-owned halls, private halls, living at home, private flats and houses – and then tackles the practical issues, from dealing with landlords to avoiding council tax, that you might face while living away from home at uni.

Halls of residence

The first decision to make is whether to live in university halls or 'live out' – which means living in a house or flat owned by a private landlord. At first glance, halls might seem like a more

TIP

'Be prepared for lots to go on when you're living in halls. We often had fire alarms at 4am – once one went off after the freshers' ball the night before, and everyone came out in their ball gowns. One of my friends kept overflowing the bath and that triggered the fire alarm for some reason too. My overriding memory of first year is running out of my room half-dressed because of fire alarms!'
Hannah, 21, Oxford

expensive option, but remember that your rent bill in halls will usually include extras like utility costs, your internet provision, and a regular cleaner, and you'll usually be able to pay to live there only during term time – so you'll be paying for fewer weeks. There will be other bonuses like access to a bar, and common room with a TV, and sometimes a catered canteen. By contrast, if you opt to live in private accommodation, you'll usually have to pay for a twelve-month contract, even if uni runs for less time, and will have to pay extra for bills, TV licence, and do your own cleaning. So be aware of what's included in the cost if price is a major concern.

Most freshers choose to live in university-owned halls of residence for their first year at uni. I did – and it was the ideal choice. Living in halls means that everything you need is on-site, from hundreds of like-minded freshers to launderettes and social events. There are practical advantages too, like not having to focus on admin – you usually only have to pay one bill, since utility bills and broadband internet are included.

The cost of living in halls will depend on where you're living and what's included in your rent, but according to the NUS, the average student rents lie between £40 and £100 a week. It can be a lot more – mine was £137 a week, but I had short, eight-week terms and I didn't have to pay for my room during the holidays so that made it a little cheaper over the course of the year.

To see what other students are paying for their accommodation you can use the rent comparison tool on the NUS website. Go to www.nus.org.uk, then click on Info, then Housing, to find a table providing detailed comparable rents in areas around the UK, divided up into catered and self-catered halls, en-suite and private housing costs.

Which halls should I go for?

Most universities own at least some halls of residence – and these are usually the cheapest option for accommodation – but there will still be other options to look into. For example, you'll still have to decide whether you want self-catered or catered halls. Self-catering is cheaper, but obviously you'll have to pay more to buy food through the year. If you enjoy cooking, this can be a fun way to meet like-minded friends. But if you're already worried about coping away from home, catered halls could be a better option. OK, so the food's unlikely to pass Gordon Ramsay's muster (frankly, Riley, even my eats-everything Labrador, wouldn't have been impressed by the nut roast that was regularly served in my halls), but you'll be able to easily find three meals a day of cheap grub surrounded by hundreds of other freshers. Even so, you should think about your own lifestyle before making the decision: if you know that you'll be getting out of bed at midday

'It's really important to look into your halls of residence – I regret my choice. It wasn't the end of the world, but I'd recommend thinking about your decision as it can impact your first year a lot.'
Howard, 22, Bristol

'If you don't ask, you don't get – so if there's something you want for your uni room, like furniture or equipment, ask your hall manager if they have one before shelling out yourself. I was given a heater and a fridge this way – after all my friends had gone out and paid for theirs.'
Kat, 20, London

every day and out every night, paying for meals that you'll always miss will make catered halls a false economy.

Since most students end up living in a flat or house in their following years, remember that there will be plenty of time to cook then, so don't let that decision put you off catered halls. But having said that, if you have any special religious or medical diet requirements – or you're just plain fussy, like me – then catered halls could be a mistake.

If you do go for self-catering accommodation, ask how many students share each kitchen, and look into the available cooking facilities. Are they clean and safe? And is there a hob, oven, freezer, microwave?

Another choice is en-suite versus shared bathrooms. This might seem like a no-brainer – if you can have your own bog, why not? But the extra cost of en-suite doesn't really make it worth it. I'm a total princess and I coped fine without en-suite accommodation. Having your own sink is really useful, even though about half of them have urine stains as a reminder of the time a drunk teenage boy couldn't be bothered to walk to the toilet – but as long as there are plenty of toilets and shower facilities to share, an en-suite bathroom isn't important – and will put a lot of extra cost on your rent bill.

> 'If you suspect your halls aren't exactly what you were hoping for, complain! Too many people settle for a bad situation.'
> Colin, 23, London

In some areas, there are also private, 'luxury' halls developments offered by companies like Unite, Cosmopolitan and Jarvis UPP. These usually have more modern designs and better facilities, such as flat-screen TVs, concierge receptions, swipe card doors rather than keys, and en-suite bathrooms, but are way more expensive.

Whichever you choose, check that whoever runs or owns your accommodation has signed up to a code of practice that will make sure the accommodation passes muster. You can check on two online lists. One, a list of accommodation managed by universities that have signed a quality charter, is available at UUK: www.universitiesuk.ac.uk/acop. For the remaining halls providers – like private halls or smaller colleges' halls – you can check ANUK's list at www.anuk.org/largecode.

Private housing

Most unis only offer halls accommodation for first years, but in any case it can be nice to have the opportunity to live with friends, cook, clean, live closer to the centre of town, and spend days arguing about whose turn it was to pick up the 'Andrex' tab. (Not mine, by the way; I bought it last week.) As a lesson in life experience, I'd recommend living out.

Living in a shared house or flat is an amazing experience. As one of my friends explains, 'Once I'd lived in my flat with five

'When you're sorting out accommodation, try to get a list of recommended landlords from your union – if you go through an agency they charge additional fees – and the two landlords that I found without using an agency were a million times better than the one I found through an agency.'
Sophie, 22, London

guys for a month, I thought, never again will I be able to live in a place where a mould colony is cultivated in the toaster and, instead of cleaning it, we put it on the kitchen table and laugh at its development!' Unsurprisingly, he was keen to remain anonymous. But if you're now hoping that you're not allocated a room in his flat, don't worry: he's just graduated.

Renting a house or flat privately means paying extra for utilities, which will add about £10–15 extra per week, plus there is extra hassle – like pleasing those nit-picking housemates who want to split water bills by the drop. You'll usually also have to shell out for a twelve-month tenancy, while in halls you can usually pay for term-time rent only.

Property hunting

If you decide to rent a house or flat, you need to start looking for properties. There are two ways to do this: through an agent, or directly, through a landlord. If you decide to use an accredited estate agent, you'll have more of assurance about a property's condition and management. Check that your agent is approved by one of the following industry bodies: RICS, ARLA, NALS or NAEA.

Most student accommodation comes under the description of a 'house in multiple occupancy' under the Housing Act 2004.

This requires landlords to be licensed and you can report them to the local authority if they fail to meet minimum standards. Ask your university housing officer or student union for more information, as the rules differ according to the type of property.

Many universities provide students with a list of all the approved houses for rent in student towns, so find out about this through your Students' Union, or ask at your uni's administrative offices. Most unis will have an accommodation office who will be able to help out if you are struggling to find private accommodation or if something has gone wrong with a landlord. They will be able to provide loads of advice on housing, and will have expert knowledge about your campus area, so are a useful first port of call.

If you decide to find a private landlord directly, you can save agency fees but may face a lot more hassles and fewer assurances about getting your deposit back (more on that later). So if you do opt for this, it's a good idea to ask older students for recommendations about landlords or properties to avoid renting a hovel from a fraudster. If you don't know anyone, ask your student union for help.

A property-hunting check list

When viewing a property, make sure you're safe – avoid going alone. Or, if you really have to go on your own, tell a friend where you are and when you expect to be back. Stay between the agent and the door in case you need to make a fast exit.

Safety checks

▶   Carbon Monoxide poisoning, which is mainly caused by faulty gas appliances, has affected thousands of students, and can result in death. Landlords must have gas appliances checked every year by a registered engineer – make sure yours does this by requesting a copy of the safety check record.

TIP

'Expect to learn as you go along – and not just about academic stuff! During my first year living in a house up at uni, we had problems with our boiler so our landlord gave us the details of our account to phone up British Gas. When the man came to look at it, he stood there for one second and then turned around to me and said, "So, you don't know how to turn on a boiler then, do you?" I'd never had to use a boiler before so why should I have known!?'
Sophie, 22, Manchester

▶ Ensure that there are smoke detectors with working batteries throughout the property.

▶ There should also be a fire blanket in the kitchen.

▶ Furnishings should have a label to prove that they are made from fire-resistant fabrics.

▶ Check that there is a safe way to escape the building in an emergency.

Location

Location is one of the most important things to think about when choosing a house or flat. Back road or busy road? I wanted to live on a main road because I felt safer coming home late at night in a place where there are lots of people, and – as a Londoner – the noise didn't bother me. Other people might feel differently.

Central or suburban? It's nice to be in the centre of town if you go out a lot, but if all your friends are living in a suburban bit, that area will probably become the centre of your life anyway so it's best to live there. Likewise, if your friends are of the cardboard-backed, paper-filled variety (that's a description of a book, duh), then a location near the library will save you loads of time.

Other things you might want to be near include the main campus, faculty buildings, clubs, cafés and supermarkets – especially if you're self-catering and don't have a car. Remember that spending a bit more money on being where you want to spend most of your time means that you'll save money on transport costs (and avoid wasting loads of time travelling) during the year.

Rent

Ask what is included in the rent (and look out for extra fees that come about through provisos in your contract, like internet download limits).

Frankly, you usually get what you pay for with accommodation. A too-good-to-be-true price probably means that the 'en-suite' aspect of your room description is a leaking ceiling in the corner of your bedroom being regarded as a shower.

Spending a bit more is often worth it in terms of happiness – you don't need a super deluxe pad that Victoria Beckham would live in, but nor do you want to be living in a stinking, damp dump that you never want to return to at the end of the day.

What should be included?

In your bedroom, expect to see a working radiator, desk, chair, bed, cupboard and light.

The exception is if your property comes 'unfurnished' – if it does, be aware of what you're going to have to spend on kitting out a room to your own standards before signing on the dotted line.

Check whether some rooms have better facilities than others – in my house, for example, the one double bed was the most desirable feature, so you should discuss with your housemates whether you're going to want to make one room's rent more expensive than another, if the landlord hasn't already done so. Make sure you have this discussion before deciding who's going to get which room – it saves lots of arguments. Although, having said that, before moving into my student house, we followed exactly this plan, and randomly drew our names out of a hat for each room, but I still got the downstairs room, and still had a sulk, so I can't promise that this method will make everyone happy!

What to look out for outside a property

- ► Broken guttering
- ► Rotten timber (on window frames and doors)
- ► Somewhere outside to store rubbish
- ► If the house or flat has a garden, ask who is responsible for looking after it.
- ► Bike storage, or parking if relevant.

What to look out for inside a property

- ► Check appliances like the fridge, cooker and oven are fully functional
- ► Look out for damp and mould
- ► Check whether electrical wiring has been safety-inspected in the last five years
- ► Look for any damage like cracks on plug sockets
- ► Check whether windows have locks
- ► Ask whether previous tenants have all returned their keys.

▶ Ask for test certificates for gas, electricity, heating and any other services.

Speak to the current residents

Try to find out who the current resident is in the house or flat, and grill them all about it. The day after we moved into our house we found it was a popular nightly meeting spot for the local tramp population.

Ask the current incumbents whether the house or flat is noisy, and whether it has a good water supply. Is the landlord or managing agent efficient, and easy to contact? Any problems with neighbours? Have they had any problems with the property while they've lived there?

Write a list of questions in advance so you don't forget anything.

Other questions

Look into disabled access and wheelchair accessibility, if necessary. And find out whether kitchens are adapted for religious requirements if required.

Signing the contract

Before signing any kind of contract you should ask someone who is responsible and experienced – parents or even a lawyer – to read through the contract to check that it is acceptable. Make sure you read it too, to find out everything about your responsibilities in your potential new home. You should especially be aware of exactly what will happen if one of your housemates leaves or falls behind on rent payments – some contracts may ask the remaining students to shell out the extra money.

Be aware that when you sign a contract to rent a property, you'll usually have to stump up for fees straight away – like a

TIP

'If something breaks, get it fixed fast – either through the halls' maintenance team or your landlord. I didn't do this in my first year, and when a fire alarm went off I ended up having to climb out of a third-storey window because my so-called best friend had broken the lock on my door a few days earlier (whilst drunkenly trying to wake me up at 3am for fun...), I'd forgotten to get it fixed and this time it had stuck.'
Tim, 21, Oxford

deposit and the first month's rent, and maybe an agent's fee too. Before you pay up, ask for an inventory list of everything that's in your property, as well as written assurance that things like the boiler and central heating system work and are regularly serviced. And if you have rented directly from a private landlord, check whether they are signed up to the Tenancy Deposit Scheme for Regulated Agents (visit www.tds.gb.com). Note that landlords are only allowed to raise rents when you're renewing your tenancy. Take photos so that you have a record of the condition of the property and its furniture, fixtures and fittings. These can be very useful if the landlord claims that you have damaged the property, such as stained carpets, or broken furniture, at the end of your tenancy.

Moving in

On the day that you move in to your new house or flat, take more photos of the property, especially any areas that are damaged – even if the damage seems minor, such as flaking paintwork or a dented cupboard. If possible, get the date digitally stamped on the photo. Taking these measures now and after signing the contract should help you to get your deposit back at the end of your tenancy period.

If you do have problems with your landlord

Try to build up a good relationship with your managing agent or landlord – if you show them that you're responsible and reliable tenants from the word go, then they will be much more likely to be sympathetic and helpful if you need something from them in the future.

'Don't feel that you have to become too aloof just cos you've started uni – don't forget your old school friends, they are still your closest buddies and are just at the other end of a phone.'
Jamie, 21, Birmingham

But problems can still crop up. For example, if you think you're going to be unable to meet your rent payments, don't try to bluff your way out of it – the landlord will see through your excuses. Be honest. You can find more advice by visiting or contacting a Citizens' Advice Bureau (www.citizensadvice.org.uk).

Most tenancies are 'Assured Shorthold' tenancies, which means that if the landlord tries to put up your rent on renewal date, you should speak to your union about appealing. Otherwise, you can appeal to the Rent Assessment Panel for either a reduction or a smaller increase. If you do go down this route, you need proof that the rent increase is unreasonable – so find comparable examples of similar houses or flats in the same kind of area and size and facilities with cheaper rents. Check out the Rent Assessment Panel's website at www.rpts.gov.uk. They also have more advice on sorting out problems with residential property. The NUS also recommend asking letting agents whether they belong to the Dispute Resolution Service, which offers extra guarantees for deposit security.

Be aware that at the end of the tenancy, landlords aren't allowed to penalise you for 'fair wear and tear' of things like carpet and appliances. If the carpet was already stained and getting on a bit and you add one more stain, you shouldn't be held accountable for the cost of a new one.

Cleaning

Be aware that landlords will want you to keep their property clean. In my house, that wasn't easy since we lived with two boys who seemed to have never lived anywhere without their mums being ten steps behind picking up everything they dropped on the floor – but we tried. We girls neatly coloured in a cleaning rota, and stuck it to the fridge, and – while I hate to perpetrate gender stereotypes, this is true – the boys just as neatly ignored it. Still, the one thing that kicked them into shape was the threat of a visit from our landlord – legally, they can visit but normally have to give notice, which in most contracts is 24 hours.

Living with people

Sharing a house or flat isn't always easy. You're bound to have lots of fun and make friends with whom you can reminisce about student days decades later, but the toxic combination of people, bills and shared toilet roll (see 'The Loo Roll Wars', below) means there are bound to be arguments too.

There are ways to lessen household tension. First, if you're choosing your housemates, think carefully. Have a snoop round their current house, if possible – if it's a stinking mess, can you cope with that? If it's obsessively tidy, are they going to be able to deal with you not cleaning up your cereal bowl as soon as you slurp the last bit of milk? Is an eight-girl house a good idea? Do you want a house with ten bedrooms or a flat with two?

TIP

'*I was disappointed to discover that flatmates can be just flatmates rather than friends – but if that happens to you too, don't worry; there are plenty of other ways to find friends at uni. I was also amazed at how different so many people in one place could be!*'
Rebecca, 22, Edinburgh

Once you've moved in, bills will be a big concern – carefully consider about how you're going to split them; see more in 'Paying bills', below. Privacy will be another issue, so set out a code from the start. Two of my friends who share a flat have innocuous-looking magnets stuck to their doors – they each know that if the magnet has gone, they shouldn't go into each other's rooms. Agree with your housemates that you won't enter each other's bedrooms when you're not there.

In the kitchen, talk about what's going to be accepted – you might want to all share food, you might want to all have separate food, you might want to share some items – but whatever you decide, stick to it. And if you do borrow someone's milk (or, worse, dip into their chocolate stash), remember to replace it as quickly as possible. Be generally considerate – don't have the heating on at a sweltering temperature to do Bikram yoga if you're sharing the heating bill, don't spend half a morning in the shower and don't slam the door late at night.

Have rules about guests – you won't want anyone's boyfriend or girlfriend moving in without a house discussion first, and it'll probably be banned in your tenancy agreement anyway. (That's a good excuse to remember if you can't stand the person, anyway.)

Don't get too stressed about the house. Keep it in as good a condition as you can, but what's student accommodation for if you can't have a party now and then without having to worry about your mum's great-aunt's antique porcelain vase being smashed? The house I shared during my second year of uni had vomit-coloured carpet, bits of the ceiling would regularly fall down and land on our heads, and the kitchen chairs had legs which fell off (regularly) whenever you sat down. But that inspired some genius games of musical chairs.

Paying bills

Most students have a bit of a shock on discovering the cost of gas, water and electricity. I stopped moaning about my family home being cold on the first weekend I went home to my parents after living in my student house – now I really do know what dad was shouting about when he'd yell that spending half an hour in the shower was a waste of money.

Bills you can expect to see dropping on a doormat near you include: telephone/internet bill, gas and electricity bill, water bill and TV licence. Some of these might come together in a 'bundle', e.g. gas and electricity, phone, digital TV and internet.

We found the best way to pay bills was by making each housemate responsible for one of them. We registered that bill in his or her name and made them responsible for paying it on time and then getting the balance back from each housemate.

Note that students don't have to pay council tax, but the council might not know you're students and will send you a bill anyway. If that happens, it's best to phone up the council as soon as possible so they can cancel your bill. It's important to pay all bills as soon as they're received, because otherwise they tend to get more expensive – with things like disconnection and reconnection fees slapped on late payers of phone bills, for example.

The Loo Roll Wars

I'd recommend that you consider having a collective kitty for things like washing-up liquid and toilet roll – after my experience living in a student house involved an ongoing argument later named 'The Loo Roll Wars'. It happened after a few months of everyone complaining that they were the only one who bought any bog roll. One day, each housemate claimed that they had bought the most recent stash, and everyone refused to buy more. We each ended up sneaking into the loo with our own tissues. It lasted an embarrassingly long time – but eventually we got over it… Still, I'd recommend the kitty option.

Making the most of your room

Having a relaxing, homely room at uni is really important – and while you can't always pick your room, you can make the most of it. If you're living in halls, make friends with the handymen – they often have a stash of furniture hidden away that they're happy to dole out if they like you! I nabbed myself a table and an extra desk that I spotted hidden in a storage area of college – and then bought some cheap material to use as a desk cover and tablecloth. It was blue gingham, so kind of reminiscent of my primary school uniform, but it was really cheap and brightened up the room.

'Take lots of postcards, posters, photos and fairy lights – it's a really good way to brighten up your room and make you feel at home.'
Ellen, 21, Edinburgh

Another idea that can economically transform your room is buying a coloured lightbulb for a decorative lamp (but stick with a normal bulb on your desk lamp to work with). Or cover the walls with photos, posters, concert tickets, postcards, messages from friends – anything that makes your room feel like home. Be careful about dictatorial landlords or hall managers, though – they have an unhealthy hatred of pins and 'Blu-tack', so check where you're allowed to put things up on the wall.

Having a plant or two can brighten up the room, and it's nice to feel responsible for it! I had a basil plant that looked lovely, until I ate it all in a pasta sauce. Other unusual decorative ideas in my friends' rooms included a paper chain made out of receipts, walls plastered with free posters from the freshers' fair, and birthday cards strung across the room on a washing line.

Washing: a simple guide...

To many newbies living away from home for the first time, Washing Your Own Clothes is a spectre so terrifying that going naked, wearing reeking clothes or – and this is something I have to shamefully admit to – buying new underwear from Primark rather than washing the old ones, can seem preferable. But despite appearances – like how much parents huff and puff when you bring mounds of stinky washing home to dump in their capable hands every holiday – washing is not that hard. Here are some quick tips to lighten the burden...

TIP

'Take at least two sets of towels – then you always have one set whilst you wash the other. The same is true for bed linen.'
Dani, 20, London

'Pack an airer to dry washing on – saves money on laundry.'
Danny, 20, Warwick

▶ Buy washing powder in tablet form rather than powder – it's less likely to dribble out the packet.

▶ Remove tissues, £5 notes and 'Gummy Bears' from pockets.

▶ Try not to mix coloured clothes with white ones.

▶ The detergent will either go directly into the drum (the massive hole where you shove all your clothes) or a dinky pull-out draw – have a good stare at the machine and you'll work out which one it is.

▶ Don't overfill the machine – your clothes will come out less clean but more crumpled. And I've never met a student who does ironing...

▶ After you've put the clothes in the machine, added the detergent and popped in some fabric conditioner (if you're feeling flush), twizzle the washing machine's knobs to 'normal' wash at about 40 degrees, unless you're an expert and can deal with another setting.

▶ Go to pick up your washing on time – set an alarm on your phone; otherwise someone else will probably remove it, with a little less love than you might put in, and drop it on the dirty floor.

▶ Don't thrust everything in the tumble drier – delicate clothes, and things like tights, will shrink. Hand dry these by hanging them up. Hang up shirts, too, and to get rid of creases hang the shirts up in the bathroom while you're having a shower – the steam will work a treat, as Mum might say.

Living at home

Unless living at home involves a transatlantic commute (obviously that sounds ridiculous, but someone I knew at uni literally did commute from New York to Oxford…) living at home will usually be the cheapest accommodation option. And there are benefits. It's free, unless your parents want a contribution towards rent, food or bills – and even if they do, it'll probably still be cheaper. There will be home-cooked meals on the table when you come home from your long day in the library, or your long night out clubbing, as it may be. And the washing machine will probably be a lot nearer your room.

But there are downsides, too. You'll probably feel a bit left out when all your uni friends are getting ready for a night out together, or bonding over mutual whinges about the lack of hot water in their halls. Unless one of your parents happens to be the university dean and you live on campus, it'll probably be a longer commute into lectures and it'll be harder to go out at night if you're living at home. There'll be higher transport costs for things like taxis, too.

If you do choose – or are financially compelled – to live at home, try to agree some ground rules with your parents to ease the situation. Tell them that you'll be considerate about coming in late, and ask them to not set a curfew. Ask them to treat you differently from the days when dad picked you up from the school disco in year 7.

But if you're telling your parents not to treat you like a kid, realise that in return you'll unfortunately have to stop acting like one. So quit leaving your shopping sprawled around the stairs when you come in, and offer to make dinner now and then. You might face the problem that, to you, sitting at the desk all day reading is working, but to them it's what they do

74

when they finish work, and they'll try to fill your day with babysitting and so on. So ensure that your parents know to leave you to study and don't ask you to do errands while you're studying. Friends who lived at home during uni tell me this kind of agreement is easier if you offer to do chores when you're not studying...

As for socialising, keep your ear to the ground about any events, be an active user of social network sites like Facebook and MySpace and the Students' Union site, ask friends to remember to keep you in the loop, and keep up with your 'home' friends too. Try to encourage your new uni friends to make the trek to your house now and then – they'll probably appreciate the home atmosphere. Lastly, don't moan to your uni friends about having no money – it won't go down well when your lack of cash has meant you've had to take a top back to H&M, while to them poverty means eating an out-of-date discounted 'Pot Noodle' for three dinners in a row.

Chapter 4

Health

At uni, with work, socialising and looking after yourself, you've got more to do than ever before, so you kind of hope that lurgies will stay away just because they'll see how busy you are. Unfortunately, they don't. The good news is that in the experience of my friends and I, the bugs tended to wait until after you'd handed in your big coursework assignment before knocking you back for six. The bad news is, in your itsy bitsy uni room there's no mum around to give sympathetic pats or endless cups of hot 'Ribena'. Sometimes there's not even a TV in the room to indulge in daytime re-runs of *ER*.

So here's a guide to keeping well and – if that goes wrong – to helping yourself to get better when you're living away from home at uni.

Before you go

New students are advised to have the MMR jab (a three-in-one measles, mumps and rubella vaccination) before arriving at university, since students are common victims of measles and mumps, especially freshers who live in close contact with

'Check you've had your second dose of MMR, as well as the one you might have had as a baby, or you may be spending your first term – or your holiday back at home – getting mumps and watching your face swell up.'
Mike, 22, Hull

hundreds of other students. You'll have to have two jabs of the vaccine (though most people had one as a baby) to be fully immunised.

You should also be vaccinated against meningitis C. If you're a sufferer of asthma who uses inhaled steroids, or have a serious long-term condition such as kidney disease, you should also have an annual flu vaccination.

Registering at a doctor and dentist

It's a really good idea to register at a doctor or dentist in your university town, so that if you fall ill and need to book a visit, they can have your notes to hand and know your medical history. You should be especially quick to register with a doctor if you have a pre-existing health condition, since you might need repeat prescriptions or similar help.

Most universities have medical centres on campus that will be used to registering students and will have the forms readily available. At others, the Students' Union and university admin officers will be able to point out the NHS surgery that is affiliated with the university.

Student surgeries will usually provide free medical certificates, and organise nurse drop-in clinics for services like vaccines, contraception and sexual health advice and general health advice. Doctors can't help with dental problems, so you should register with a dentist who is near uni too.

A recent NUS survey found that one in ten students don't visit their doctor with health concerns because they're worried about the cost, and 10% of students aren't even registered with a doctor at all. So remember that it's usually free to register and visit a GP, and most students qualify for free or reduced prescriptions, eye tests and dental checks, too. You can apply for help with health costs, including prescriptions and dental care, through the HC1 form, available from most surgeries and pharmacies.

Avoiding illness

You probably learnt about this as a three-year-old, but just as GCSE revision notes flew out of the brain faster than Formula One on fast-forward, you probably don't remember all of these tips either. Here are some simple precautions to help prevent the spread of many of the viral lurgies and illnesses.

▶ If you cough or sneeze, that spreads disease, so use a tissue and chuck it down the loo, then flush the chain.

▶ If friends or housemates are ill, stay away. If you do hang out with them, wash your hands frequently, with soap.

▶ Wash your cups, cutlery and crockery in hot, soapy water after using them. If someone not too hygiene-happy has used them before you, it's a good idea to wash up before you use dishes and cutlery, too.

What to do if you feel ill: ice cream, jelly and telly

If you're feeling a bit dodgy but not desperately ill, you can probably cope with treating yourself – tell someone to keep an eye on you, and go to bed if you're feeling rubbish. Pour some hot water into a bowl and breath in the steam if you've got a bad cold, or dip into the well-stocked medical resources that your parents probably packed for you if you think you need some pharmaceutrical help.

Take a dose of paracetamol or ibuprofen for a headache, for example, or use another remedy for coughs, colds and sore throats. Remember to read and follow the instructions on the label. Make hot drinks with honey for a sore throat. And if you're living in a single room, it's a good idea to tell someone like a neighbour if you're feeling at all bad, so they can check up on you and make sure you're OK.

If you cut yourself, don't wipe the blood on your jeans and ignore it – cuts can get infected, so wash the injury, put on some anti-bacterial cream like 'Savlon', and pop on a plaster.

If it's a bit more serious...

If you'd like a bit more expert advice, take a visit to the local pharmacist, who can give advice on complaints like colds, coughs, flu, sore throats and other aches and pains. They'll be able to tell you if they think you should visit your GP.

You could also give NHS Direct a ring on 0845 4647. This is a confidential, 24-hour advice and health information service staffed by nurses. They can help out if you're feeling bad and need advice, as well as give details of local health services like your nearest GP, dentist or out-of-hours pharmacy.

Is there a doctor in the house?

Another health destination is your local GP surgery or student health centre. They'll provide everything you've come to expect from the local doctor – a long queue, and a surly receptionist – no, just joking. Maybe. But they will be able to provide you with medical treatment, prescriptions, specialist or hospital referrals, injections and tests.

I need help and I need it now!

If you've got a medical emergency, call 999. The time to call 999 is if someone is unconscious or bleeding heavily, if you suspect someone – including yourself – may have a broken bone, a deep cut or laceration, or serious chest pain, or are having difficulty breathing. Call a friend or neighbour too, so they can wait with you and give directions to the paramedics if necessary.

Sometimes it may be appropriate to go to your nearest hospital Accident & Emergency ward, but you are able to get there without an ambulance. Either way, if you're injured or seriously ill, you should go, or be taken, to A&E. Major A&E departments are open every hour and day of the year – but note that not all hospitals have A&E departments so find out where your nearest one is just in case you need it. Some hospitals have other services available on site, such as walk-in centres and minor injury units, which are for patients without an appointment.

First aid

Most unis run first aid courses, or you can contact the St. John's Ambulance organisation to find one in your area.

You'll learn skills like how to save a life – which, let's be honest, is a lot more important than next month's essay on the use of the pronoun in Marx's *Das Kapital*. You'll also meet new people in the process. If you sign up as a St John's volunteer after the course, you can also get cool freebies like tickets to footie matches, festivals and concerts if you agree to work for some of the time.

If you're feeling down, talk to someone

Four out of five people between 18 and 21 know someone who has experienced a mental health problem – so it's a good idea to find out if your university has a counselling service, just in case you need it for you or a friend in the future. It will often be able to offer advice on debt, mental health, legal and housing issues as well as personal problems and relationship advice.

'If your parents want to come and visit, let them – don't be embarrassed. They'll probably take you out for a nice meal, buy you lots of 'essential' things you need, and may even sort your washing that week!'
James, 23, Cambridge

There will usually be other options too, like a Student Union-run counselling service, and personal tutors who will each have a group of students to look after. The helpfulness of this tutor will depend on who you are given – some will rival Phil and Fern's pastoral skills, fully trained and fascinated in your life; others will be more like Simon Cowell. If yours isn't helping you, try to swap to a new one – contact your course organisers or faculty office to find out if it's possible.

Most unis also have chaplains, who'll be trained to give advice for religious (as well as non-religious) students. Many also have 'parenting' or mentoring schemes – at mine we were each allotted a student 'family': a 'mum' and 'dad' who were second years doing our subject, plus a 'brother' and 'sister' who were fellow freshers.

Homesickness

Sometimes – especially at the start of uni – it can seem like everyone else is having a better time than you, or there aren't any people that are your 'type', or you miss your family and friends at home, or you just feel like you want to cry. These feelings are absolutely normal and will usually fade as you get into uni life.

It's a good idea to keep busy, and don't forget that everyone else is in the same boat – even when their Facebook status says they are having THE TIME OF THEIR LIVESSSSSSS, they are probably having wobbly moments inside. When my friends

'Don't feel pressured by freshers' week. I know a gazillion people love it, but I found it a little terrifying with a sense that "Oh my goodness, if I don't go out THIS VERY MINUTE then I will never make any friends ever and they will all have nicknames and the World Will End." The truth is, it really doesn't, and whilst it is a good idea to talk to people and be social it's OK if you want to take an early night or go nap/read/eat chocolate for a bit.'
Charlotte, 22, London

and I were in our second year at uni, and started to talk about freshers' week, I discovered that my most confident-seeming, taking-it-in-his-stride friend had been spending every evening crying on the phone to his mum.

If you do feel upset, confide in a new friend (or even a total stranger – there's nothing like tears to bond a new friendship), or call home if you feel like it. If you want more expert advice, there will usually be a peer support team in place at the Students' Union, as well as a Night Line that you can call if you feel sad or depressed in the night. Universities will also have student advice centres, often in the campus medical centre. The counsellors, doctors and nurses there will be used to hearing about homesickness, and will be able to offer support and advice, plus medicine if they think it will help you out.

Stress

A bit of stress can be OK – light stressing about a course deadline, for example, will help you to work hard and do your best. But if stress starts to feel overwhelming, and develops into symptoms like making you feel irritable a lot of the time, or have trouble sleeping, or develop a lot of headaches, or you start to feel dizzy or lose your appetite, you might want to think about how you can reduce your stress. This is equally true if you keep feeling sudden blasts of dry mouth, butterflies in your stomach, a pounding heart, sweating or shortness of breath.

Take some steps to sort out the root source of stress – if an essay deadline is impossible to meet, talk to tutors. If a boyfriend or girlfriend is getting you down, think about what you want from the relationship. See if you can change your circumstances to ease your feeling of unhappiness.

Aim for a good life balance – so that's a diet with lots of exercise and enough sleep, not too much boozing, and a good

> *'Bring board games like Scrabble, Cluedo, Monopoly – they're a really social thing to do when you're too tired to go out.'*
> Rosie, 20, Edinburgh

amount of both working and studying. A friend and I signed up to a yoga course to alleviate stress during a time when we had tons of work. I was terrible at yoga, and couldn't stop laughing at my inability to do, well, any of the moves, which made the teacher surprisingly mad at me – but the laughing session was just as de-stressing as yoga is supposed to be.

Again, if everything feels like it's getting too much, find some expert help.

Students with disabilities

Going to uni is a huge deal anyway, but if you have any kind of impairment, like physical, learning or mental health difficulties, it can seem harder when your home support bases are further away. Here's a guide to the kinds of support – be they academic, social or financial – that you might be eligible for if you are disabled, plus info on where to look for further guidance.

The Disability Discrimination Act and uni support

Part four of this Act ensures that universities have to carry out 'reasonable adjustments' to make sure that disabled students are not 'substantially disadvantaged'. The kind of support that you might need or want within those loose lines of guidance will vary. Speak to your uni's learning support team or disability officer before you arrive on campus, if possible, because he or she will be able to sort out any help that'll make your life easier. To get the disability officer's contact details, go to the Skill (the National Bureau for Students with Disabilities) website – www.skill.org.uk/education – where you'll find details of disability advisors on campuses across the UK. Or contact Skill on 0800 328 5050, via Textphone on 0800 068 2422, or email them at info@skill.org.uk.

If you want to talk to an older student in a similar position on campus get in contact with the Students with Disabilities rep at the Students' Union.

Some support ideas that unis might make available to help you include: extra time or rest breaks during exams; the use of a laptop, voice recorder, reader or a scribe; pre-term time to get used to campus; a support worker; booklists in advance for transcription; longer book loans; an induction loop in study rooms; a flashing light or vibrating pad for the fire alarm; designated parking spaces; staff awareness of your disability; and wheelchair-accessible classrooms, toilets and other rooms.

Funding support through the disabled student's allowances

There are a few different allowances and each covers different types of extra costs that you're incurring at uni because of your disability. There's a general allowance (up to £1,680) for things like extra photocopying or extra book-buying; one for specialist equipment like computer gear or furniture, that's capped at £5,030 for the duration of your course; another allowance to cover the wages of a support worker or personal assistant, up to £20,000 a year for full-time students (or £15,000 for

part-timers); and an allowance for extra travel costs too.
Find out more at www.direct.gov.uk/en/DisabledPeople.

While it's true that all universities should have a written policy
statement on how they accommodate students with disabilities,
they might not have thought about someone with your personal
needs – so it's important to visit unis before confirming your
application (or at least before confirming a place) to make sure
that you can live and study on campus safely and happily.

Booze, drugs, rock and roll...

Let's be honest – unless you've made a conscious decision to
be teetotal at university, you're probably going to spend a bit of
it drunk. I know this, because before uni I didn't drink much
at all, and while I didn't go OTT just because I'd become a
student, I did get drunk at times, like at balls and birthdays, but
I never got so drunk that I didn't know where I was or who
I was with or how I'd get home. Frankly, I'm too much of a
control freak for that to seem like fun.

And it is important that you don't go out and get absolutely
bladdered all the time, for lots of reasons. First, your friends
won't be very impressed if every time you all go out they end up
having to look after you or bring you home early while mopping
up your vomit and making apologetic noises to an apoplectic
taxi driver. Secondly, it's pretty dangerous. Short term, it damages
your concentration and puts you at risk of things like date rape
and car crashes and unprotected sex. Long term, it's even worse
– regular drinking can cause liver disease, heart attacks and
cancer. Alcohol is also stuffed full of calories and makes you fat.

So it's best to know your own limits – have a few drinks, but
not a few too many. After a big boozing session, don't drink for
another 48 hours, so your body can recover.

'Be careful about the consequences of drink...
A couple of my friends regularly enjoyed a good
drink while having a typically studenty argument
about "The Arts". During one particularly heated
exchange, one of them stormed onto the balcony
outside their halls' kitchen, slammed the door
– and broke off the handle. The rest of his friends
let him freeze for several hours in only a shirt and
the snowy November night air. They eventually
called the fire brigade to lower him down, but my
mate still got the last laugh – flirting away to get a
fireman's number!'
Victoria, 21, Oxford

How much is too much? According to NHS guidelines, men
should not regularly drink more than three to four units a day;
for women, the recommended limit is two to three units a day.
Sounds a lot – but isn't. A teeny (125ml) glass of Chardonnay is
nearly two units. It's really easy to go overboard, so be careful.

Just because the student bar, pubs and clubs are at the centre
of student life, that doesn't mean you have to get wasted
every night. Stick to soft drinks sometimes – your wallet
will appreciate it too – and suggest nights out to the cinema,
bowling – we even crashed the local OAPs' bingo hall a few
times for a classic night out.

Smoking

If you smoke, you should know that the risks include lung
cancer, heart disease, wrinkly skin, impotence, reduced sperm
count in men, reduced fertility in women, gum disease, obesity
and more cellulite. Socially, the tables are also turning against

smoking – you have to go outside to smoke in public places like pubs and restaurants. Cigarettes are expensive and being a student might make cigarettes unaffordable. If you want to find help to quit, see http://smokefree.nhs.uk/.

Drugs

Drugs can sometimes be seen as part of the student experience – but they're illegal for a reason. They involve horrible risks to your mental and physical health, and make you more likely to do stupid things like run in front of cars or have unprotected sex.

Once you're hooked on pot you're more likely to get addicted to drugs like heroin or cocaine. Cannabis users may also experience paranoia, loss of co-ordination, lung disease and lung cancer, respiratory problems such as bronchitis and asthma, high blood pressure, and infertility. Taking ecstasy can cause coma and even death. Cocaine raises blood pressure, and can bring about heart failure. Overdosing on heroin can also cause heart failure, unconsciousness and coma. So, since it's preferable to leave uni in a graduation gown rather than a stretcher, you should avoid taking drugs.

Plus, if you're found by the police with a class A drug like cocaine, you could be in prison for up to seven years. If you thought your campus food was bad, it's bound to be worse in prison. Most unis also ban people with drug convictions from campus and drop them from courses.

You can find more info on the (confidential) FRANK helpline on 0800 776 600 or at www.talktofrank.com.

Sex

Let's keep it brief. You're legal, it's legal and, hey, it's even good exercise – this isn't going to be a year 10 sex ed/abstinence lesson. But just because you're living in halls with 500 rampant teenagers doesn't mean you have to have sex with them all. It's hard enough to look after yourself, let alone a smaller, cuter but needier version of yourself, so make sure you avoid unprotected sex. Use a condom, get on the pill, or find out about other options on the crudely named www.condomessentialwear. co.uk site and stick to safe sex.

Having unprotected sex can also leave you riddled with diseases. You could catch a venereal disease, like gonorrhoea or syphilis. Other STDs include herpes, pubic lice, warts, HIV and chlamydia. Some may have symptoms, like unusual discharge from the vagina or penis, bleeding, pain or burning sensation when weeing, rashes, itching or tingling around the genitals or anus – but, scarily, some might not have any symptoms at all, so it's important to get checked.

If you haven't done already, go to a doctor or student health clinic, because some sexually transmitted diseases have no side effects. Also book a visit if your bits down below start to hurt or itch or smell or look a bit weird. Seek medical advice or phone the sexual health helpline on 0800 567 123.

Use a condom whenever you have sex to stop the transmission of most STDs – you can use them as well as another method of contraception, such as the pill, which does not protect against infections.

Exercise

It can be easy to start thinking of exercise in terms of your weekly set of calculations from your tutor, or a nightly dancing regime out clubbing. Both are good – for the brain and body – but you should also plan to incorporate regular exercise into your day. I used to cycle around campus, but my university

> **TIP**
>
> 'If you go to uni hoping to join loads of sports clubs, remember that standards are likely to be insanely high as the spread of people is far wider – it's not going to be easy to get in just because you were year 10 netball captain. So be prepared to be intimidated but also to get stuck in and search out people who are more your standard; generally they'll be there.'
> Rebecca, 23, Edinburgh

was in a bike-friendly city – I wouldn't feel as safe doing so in London, or Manchester, for example. I'd go for runs and walks when it felt like I'd been sitting at my desk all day, and I found online freebies for day passes at local posh gyms, which I'd regularly use with a friend. We'd reward a sweaty gym session with a swim and then slob around in the sauna.

Most unis have really cheap gyms and pools on campus. If you're amazing at a particular sport, join the university squad. If you're not, but love to do a particular sport, join (or start) a club where you can meet friends, have fun and burn some energy. Most unis have everything from aerobics and boxing to orienteering and trampolining.

Aim for at least half an hour's exercise, five times a week. And if you feel guilty for leaving the books behind to work out, remember that exercise is not only good for your overall health and fitness, but also boosts mental wellbeing, including keeping you calm during exams. And remember all the other steps you can take to avoid being lazy – walk to lectures instead of getting the bus, take the stairs not the escalator, kick a football around with your friends in the park, or schedule a game of tennis.

Chapter 5

Food

I was a bit of a wannabe foodie as a fresher. I arrived at uni with more than just a couple of boxes of 'Pot Noodle' – I had woks, colanders – I think there might even have been some nutmeg in the mix. But it was all a sham – hey, I said I was a *wannabe* foodie. I had great intentions about cooking every day and popping the leftovers into a 'Tupperware' for the next day's lunch, and I really intended to make big batches of soup and take out a little portion every day... But it just didn't happen. During freshers' week I got into the habit of eating food I hated in the college canteen, because I wanted to be with other people rather than stirring a saucepan of foodie goodness on my own in the kitchen.

So don't feel bad if you get into a similar pattern of eating out with friends at the start of uni. It's important to meet people, and eating is one of the best ways to bond. Absolute independence is never going to be a jam (or even a baked bean) sandwich from the word go. What is important, though, is that once you start slotting into a regular routine with lectures and sports or a job or whatever, you start thinking about what you're eating. If you follow Chapter 2's budgeting advice, this will crop up anyway – because by writing down what you're spending, you'll soon notice that eating out, and eating junk, are both expensive ways to fill up your tummy. They're also not that healthy – most freshers find their waistline growing at the same pace as money worries in those early days.

Instead, eating a balanced diet and healthy food will help you to feel better and stay healthy at university. And you don't have to pay loads to eat well – healthy ingredients like vegetables are cheaper than greasy takeaways or supermarket ready meals.

If possible, it's a good idea to have a guided tour of What To Do in the Kitchen with someone before you go. Andy, a UCL physics student, did this because he had concerns that his diet as a fresher might damage his health – he'd represented the UK in sport at an international level. 'I was really worried about eating well, so before I came to my halls of residence, I asked my dad to teach me how to cook some basic dishes,' he says. 'Learning was quite fun, and meant I wasn't forced to tuck into a ready meal every night.'

How to go food shopping

Even though I knew how to cook at home, suddenly, at uni where I was sharing a tiny kitchen with ten other students, it

> **TIP**
>
> 'Whenever you go out shopping in town, break your notes when you can – that way you'll always have change for washing machines, vending machines, and buses that only accept correct change – and change machines at uni are invariably out of order.'
> Danielle, 22, Edinburgh

all seemed a bit different. I remember my first solo supermarket shopping trip really well. I'd done supermarket sweeps before, of course, but then it had been for my whole family, and the receipt was always reimbursed… So on my first uni supermarket trip, feeling a bit clueless, I bought the same big packets of things like salad leaves, ketchup bottles and chicken that we had in the fridge at home. By the time I reached the checkout, I had to leave my bike at the store and use the last of my cash on a taxi to get back to halls, since the bulging bags were too heavy to carry.

Of course, I couldn't get through a pack of four chicken breasts before they started to smell, and the salad leaves wilted because I didn't have time to think up imaginative salads. The ketchup was all right – but since it was a big, family-sized bottle, my neighbours seemed to think that it was a communal stash – and it was drained as quickly as my bank balance after that first food shop.

But I soon got wiser. The next week, before I went shopping I sat down with my diary and wrote a list. First I wrote down the meals I'd actually be cooking for – quite often I'd eat in the halls canteen – then I thought about things like what I wanted to eat, and whether I'd be cooking for other people too. And then I wrote down the ingredients I'd need for those dishes – and only then did I actually go shopping.

Where to go food shopping

At first, I stuck to the supermarket. But then I realised I'd just been sucked into the whole loyalty card thing and wasn't actually saving money. I started discovering local markets and realised the benefit of a pre-term trip to a big 'cash and carry' with mum, dad, their car and their credit card. They weren't always willing to go along with the charade at the till that I'd 'forgotten' my wallet (again!), but by the end of three years, it didn't matter; I had become an expert at whipping up cheap, tasty, quick and healthy meals.

What to eat

The golden rule is all about balance – a bit of chocolate is fine (and, in my book, a lot is fine if you've got an essay crisis), but try to eat five portions of fruit and vegetables a day. Think about your balance of protein (in things like chicken, houmous, red meat, fish, eggs), dairy products (cheese, milk, yoghurt) and starches (bread, potatoes, rice, pasta).

Shopping list

If you're self-catering at uni, before the start of every term, do a huge food shop to buy store cupboard basics like big packets of pasta, tinned tomatoes, herbs, rice, sauces. Even the best domestic god(dess) comes back from lectures absolutely exhausted and wants nothing more than a bowl of spaghetti, a jar of pasta sauce to shove on top and a 'Babybel' broken up on top. (Believe me, the 'Babybel' is a great addition to this traditional cuisine.) By getting the basics sorted at the beginning of term, you'll have something to whip up even if you forget to go shopping. But what are basics for a single

TIP

'A tip for cooking in a hurry – how to scramble an egg in the microwave. Get two eggs, add a splash of milk, and a twist of salt and pepper into a cereal bowl and lightly whisk with a fork. Then microwave on high for about two minutes, but stop the microwave every 30 seconds; otherwise you get a massive lump of cooked egg at the end.'
Danni, 21, Surrey

student cook? Luckily, here's a list I made earlier – add any ingredients you especially like, take away any you can't stand, and away you go…

Store cupboard

▶ Big pack of pasta

▶ Big pack of rice (easy cook is, er, the easiest)

▶ Jars of herbs – I found oregano, cumin, basil really useful – just sprinkle over some cooking vegetables and ta-da, you have an exotic(ish) sauce

▶ Soy sauce – to add to a healthy chicken or veg stir fry

▶ Stock cubes or stock powder – for making soups

▶ Ketchup – a secret ingredient in many a spaghetti Bolognese

▶ Tomato puree – a cheap and healthy pasta sauce addition

▶ Tins of tomatoes – you can never have too many tomatoes

▶ Tins of baked beans – forget about the student stereotype and enjoy – the low-salt version is pretty healthy

▶ Cans of tuna

▶ Curry paste (much cheaper than a takeaway)

▶ Packs of instant mash (if you don't have time to cook real spuds)

▶ Packs of straight-to-wok noodles (so fast, so yum, so much cheaper than Wagamama)

▶ Oil – sunflower is cheapest, olive oil is healthiest – take your pick

▶ Salt

▶ Vinegar

'Everyone uses your stuff if you leave it in communal spaces. So don't!'
Micah, 19, Oxford

Fresh and frozen ingredients

▶ Eggs

▶ Cheddar (or similar) cheese

▶ Meat (minced is cheapest)

▶ Fish (cheaper ones include trout, sardines and mackerel)

▶ Onions

▶ Tomatoes

▶ Mushrooms

▶ Cucumber and lettuce leaves – for salads and sandwich fillings

▶ Butter

▶ Bread – French baguettes are cheap, brown bread is healthy and especially yummy when toasted

▶ Bags of frozen veg – I found peas, spinach and casserole veg bags useful and cheap – they can he used to make soup, Bolognese, casserole and pasta sauces

Shopping tips

▶ Head to a bargain store like Lidl or Netto for big bulk

▶ Go to local markets for fruit and veg discounts – but don't stick too closely to your list – buy whatever is on offer that week, and adapt meals accordingly. My uni town's market used to run every Wednesday, selling ten of a particular fruit or vegetable for £1. I'd buy whatever was on offer and look up recipes online so my diet had some variety

▶ Get meat from local butchers – on some meat cuts, they're cheaper. Chicken fillets were especially cheap at my local butcher – and if you build up a rapport they often offer discounts.

▶ Be a supermarket whore – not literally – I mean, shop around. Buy from Asda one week, Sainsbury's and Tesco the next, and work out which is cheaper for your average shop.

- ▶ Near closing time, supermarkets discount their food. If you really can't be bothered to make your own sarnies, consider buying discounted ones to eat the next day. But you can't be fussy about fillings...

- ▶ If you're living in a student house, share your shopping – that way you can capitalise on offers like 'buy one get one free'. Also when things like meat and fish are on special offer, buy a bit more and freeze them until you're ready to eat them.

- ▶ Buy in season – in winter, root vegetables (like carrots) and citrus fruits (lemons, oranges – but you probably know that...) are cheaper. In summer, make the most of cheaper seasonal tomatoes, cucumbers, berries and grapes.

- ▶ Downgrade a brand to save money. One of my friends at uni swore that a supermarket's version of a particular popular cereal was the same as the (more expensive) branded version. I disagreed. He secretly switched my packet. I didn't notice. He gloated. I quietly switched to the supermarket's brand of cereal.

- ▶ Buy supermarket takeaways – if you've gotta have some ready-made food, buy your pizzas and curries from the frozen section, not the takeaway, to save cash.

- ▶ See if it's cheaper to shop online. Split the delivery charge by ordering with friends, and visit a price-comparison site like www.mysupermarket.co.uk to find the cheapest shop.

- ▶ Find easy recipes in student cook books and online at sites like www.studentcook.co.uk, where all the recipes are written and eaten by students, and free. But feel free to adapt recipes for your own taste – how else do you think the peanut butter and jelly sandwich was invented?

- ▶ If you've got a freezer, make double quantities of things like pasta sauces or curry and freeze the leftovers for lazy days.

- ▶ If you're vegetarian, make sure you eat plenty of protein – stock up on things like houmous, beans and lentils – cheap and healthy.

- ▶ Avoid campus shops – they usually sell pricey, unimaginative food.

Hygiene tips (read if you're scared of killing someone)

If you're more likely to be called a chicken than know what to do with a raw one, the kitchen can appear to be a scary place. So follow these hygiene tips.

> **TIP**
>
> 'If you want to cook but don't have many resources, like me in my first year, discover how to boil an egg in a kettle! I take no health and safety responsibility here – my mum went barmy when she discovered that I'd done this – but when I popped an egg in its shell into the kettle and switched it on, the egg cooked nicely and quickly – ready in about 5 minutes!'
> Rina, 21, London

▶ Clean. It's an important word in the kitchen. Wash your hands, with soap (apparently you're meant to wash so long that you can get through singing 'happy birthday' in your head, twice). Also wash your crockery, cutlery, saucepans, etc. in really hot water with washing up liquid.

▶ Go to war with germs with the help of cloths and anti-bacterial cleaners – spray the cleaner all over surfaces and scrub them clean with a new (or freshly washed in hot water) clean cloth.

▶ Put tea towels in the washing machine once a week, or more often if they're covered in suspicious staining.

▶ Think about how you're putting food away in the fridge – make sure it's covered, especially things like raw meat, and don't squeeze everything into one shelf – imagine each item of food needs room to breathe.

▶ Don't let raw meat or fish sit next to cooked items in the fridge.

▶ If you're cooking with raw fish or meat (especially chicken), clean all the dishes and utensils that touch the raw food really, really well. I liked to just shove it all in the sink and pour boiling water over it. A year 10 biology video left me really paranoid about raw food contamination.

▶ If you take something out of the freezer and it starts to thaw, use it up – don't put it back in the freezer. Even ice cream. As if you needed a better excuse to eat the whole tub.

▶ Make sure anything that you take out of the freezer is totally defrosted before you start to cook it. Take it out of the freezer in the morning if you're using it at night, or use a microwave to speedily defrost, but make sure you're thorough.

▶ Don't put anything warm in the fridge – if you're saving leftovers, make sure they cool first.

▶ Make sure that your fridge is set at less than 5°C.

▶ Don't store tinned leftovers (like beans or tomatoes) in their tins – they'll corrode. And metallic tomatoes don't do good things to your insides. Put them in a covered bowl or piece of 'Tupperware'.

▶ Make sure you eat foods before their sell-by date comes up – or don't wait too long afterwards... Never eat fresh meat and fish if it's out of date.

Recipes

My mum's Bolognese sauce
Can be added to pasta or rice. Makes for four, can freeze leftovers.

You'll need:

▶ 1 onion
▶ 1lb minced beef
▶ Twist of salt and pepper
▶ 3 grated carrots
▶ 4 finely chopped mushrooms
▶ A squeeze of Worcester sauce
▶ A squeeze of tomato ketchup

Fry one onion until it is soft. Add 1 lb of minced beef and fry until it is brown. Add a pinch of salt, a twist of pepper, three grated carrots, three finely chopped mushrooms, a dash of Worcester sauce and a generous squirt of tomato ketchup and cook on a medium heat for 20 minutes.

Onion soup (vegetarian)
Make up a big pot of this and eat it over a few days, or freeze any leftovers.

You'll need:

- ▶ 5 onions
- ▶ A grape-sized blob of butter
- ▶ Vegetable stock like Marigold Vegetable Bouillon
- ▶ Boiling water
- ▶ French bread and cheese (Gruyère or Cheddar work well) to serve

Thinly chop the onions and fry them in a large saucepan with a generous blob of butter. Fry until they turn dark brown (about 15 minutes) stirring them throughout. Make up two pints of vegetable stock – I use Marigold Vegetable Bouillon, where you add four teaspoons and four pints of boiling water. Pour the stock into the saucepan, bring to the boil and simmer for another 10 minutes. To serve, pour the soup into a large bowl. Float a piece of French bread on top, then place cheese on top. Melt the cheese by ladling another spoonful of soup on top.

Pasta sauce (vegetarian)
Makes enough for two (you can always add any leftovers to rice or veg for another meal).

You'll need:

- ▶ 2 tablespoons of oil (olive oil or sunflower)
- ▶ 2 chopped onions
- ▶ A peeled clove of garlic (if you've got one – or you can go without)
- ▶ 1 tin chopped tomatoes
- ▶ A twist of salt and pepper
- ▶ Grated cheese to serve

*Let the oil heat in the pan for 2 minutes, then add the chopped
onions. Fry for 5 minutes or until soft, then chop the garlic and
add it to the mix. Pour in the tin of tomatoes and stir for 5 minutes
until heated through. Add the salt and pepper, stir more. Serve
poured on top of pasta (use 100–125 grams for one person) and
grate your favourite cheese on top. For variety, you could add
chicken at the same time that you're adding the tomatoes (make
sure it's cooked throughout – it should all be white, never pink).
Or add other vegetables, like courgettes, spinach or sweetcorn.*

Stir fry
Makes enough for two.

You'll need:

- ▶ 2 tablespoons of oil (sesame oil is tastiest here, but whatever you've got will do)
- ▶ 2 chopped onions
- ▶ A bag of stir fry veg (sold in supermarkets for about 80p)
- ▶ A chicken breast (you could use beef if preferred)
- ▶ 3 tablespoons of soy sauce – or, if you're feeling flush, you can buy other varieties like Hoi Sin or Sweet and Sour for a bit of restaurant taste
- ▶ Noodles (I use the straight-to-wok variety – a bit pricier, but much easier)

*If you've bought normal noodles, you'll have to cook them in a
saucepan alongside the frying pan – check the pack to see how
long they take. With straight-to-wok noodles, you can wait till
the end. Either way, heat the oil in a big frying pan or wok for
2 minutes, then add the chopped onions. Fry for 5 minutes or until
soft, then add the bag of veg. Stir. Then add the chicken breast,
cut into pieces (an average chicken breast can be cut into about
8 pieces). Drizzle your chosen sauce on top, stir through for
2 minutes. If you've bought straight-to-wok noodles (don't worry,
woks aren't obligatory; you can cook them in a frying pan), add
them now and stir to break up the block – then eat.*

Chicken risotto
Makes enough for one.

You'll need:

- About 75g of risotto rice
- 1 chicken breast
- 1 onion
- 3 mushrooms
- 2 tablespoons of oil
- A handful of frozen (or not) peas
- A twist of salt and pepper
- 1 peeled garlic clove

Cook the rice by pouring it into a microwaveable bowl, cover with boiling water and microwave for 10 minutes. (Or do it in a saucepan if you prefer.) Chop up the chicken into small strips. Chop the onion and mushrooms and finely chop the garlic. Add them all to a saucepan with hot oil. When cooked (onions should be soft, chicken should be white throughout – cut it in half to check), add the peas. Once the rice is cooked, add it to the pan, pour in half a cup of boiling water. Keep stirring and cooking until it's all mixed, and the water has been absorbed. Add salt and pepper to taste.

My dad's main course soup (vegetarian)
Serves four.

You'll need:

- Olive oil
- 3 chopped onions
- 2 cloves of garlic
- 1 litre boiling water
- 1 tin chopped tomatoes
- Mixed herbs
- A twist of salt and pepper
- 1 tin baked beans
- 3 carrots
- 2 handfuls of frozen peas
- 2 handfuls of frozen sweetcorn

- ▶ 100g pasta
- ▶ Grated Parmesan

Pour two tablespoons of oil into a big saucepan, then add chopped onions and finely chopped garlic. Stir the onions until they're soft and brown, then add 1 litre of boiling water, 1 tin of chopped tomatoes, salt and pepper and mixed herbs. If desired, use a hand-held blender to make the soup smooth. Then add a tin of baked beans, the chopped carrots, peas, sweetcorn, and pasta. When the pasta is soft, serve in bowls topped with grated Parmesan and more mixed herbs.

Lasagna (can be vegetarian)
Makes a big dish for four.

You'll need:

- ▶ Bolognese sauce (see above – or, for a vegetarian lasagna, omit the beef and simply use the 'pasta sauce' recipe above if preferred)
- ▶ 30g butter
- ▶ 2 tablespoons of plain flour
- ▶ 400ml of milk
- ▶ 150g Cheddar
- ▶ A packet of dried lasagna pasta sheets – you'll need about 9 sheets
- ▶ 2 pinches of mustard
- ▶ Mozzarella cheese slices

First make the Bolognese sauce. Next, make the cheese sauce: melt the butter in a saucepan, then stir in the flour. Take the pan off the heat and add milk and mustard, stir for 3 minutes. Put back on a (very low) heat and stir in the cheese. If it's too thick, add more milk; too runny, add more flour. Keep stirring to avoid it going lumpy. Next, plonk the pasta sheets (carefully...) in a pan of boiling water – make sure they're not stuck together. Let them soak for about 3 minutes, until soft, then drain the water and separate the pasta sheets out on plates. Heat the oven to 200°C. Use a portion of the wrapper from a cube of butter to make the sides of an ovenproof dish greasy. Arrange a layer of pasta sheets along the bottom of the oven dish, and pour a quarter of the Bolognese sauce on top. Then make another layer of pasta sheets, and pour a quarter of the cheese sauce. Repeat until your ingredients are used up. Add some slices of Mozzarella cheese on top. Bake for 35–45 minutes – it's a good idea to wrap the dish in tin foil for the first 20 minutes, and then remove the foil to let it brown.

How to cook fish

This is a simple how-to guide – you can serve with vegetables and potatoes for an easy meal for one.

You'll need:

- ▶ 1 portion of your preferred fish (e.g. salmon, cod)
- ▶ 1 lemon (or lemon juice)
- ▶ Olive oil
- ▶ 1 clove of garlic
- ▶ Pepper
- ▶ Tin foil

Put the fish in a 'parcel' of tin foil, slice up the lemon and put it around the fish (or drizzle with lemon juice). Drizzle with oil, add the garlic and any desired extra ingredients. Wrap the fish up, leaving a small opening at the top, and bake the fish in a preheated oven at about 200°C for 20 minutes.

Chapter 6

Work

If an alien landed on earth and flicked through a stack of UCAS forms, they'd probably read about how much you love your course, how you're fascinated by the details, and how you're so excited about discovering more about ancient Mesopotamia that you find it hard to think about anything else. They would probably come to the conclusion that work is the reason we all go to uni.

Right? Hmm. By the time you start uni it can be easy to get so focused on things like what colour pins you're going to use on the pinboard in your room, and which T-shirt colour you're going to go for during the freshers' week traffic-light party, that you might forget about the reason your parents, teachers and future employers think you're at uni – to do some work.

But it will soon sink in. For me, it was halfway through my first essay of term, when I had a sudden nightmare that in my first seminar my tutor would turn to me and say, 'Sorry, we've just realised we let you in by mistake – it's best that you go home now.' I was sure I'd be exposed as the stupid one during classes among coursemates who I expected to be so clever that they'd refer to each other as 'genii'. I felt especially insecure/stupid since I had a gap year, spent alternating between writing about footballers' wives at a tabloid newspaper and travelling around on holiday – so it had been a very long time since I'd sat down and written an essay. Or read anything other than *Heat*.

From school to uni

There are lots of similarities between school and uni – campus food tastes a lot like school dinners, you cry on your first day (OK, maybe that's just me), you get excited about going to WH Smith to buy new stationery at the start of every year... But in terms of learning, there are a lot of differences: at school you get used to being told what to do every minute of the school day. At uni, you're on your own to work out which lectures are worth getting out of bed for, and when you're going to start work on assignments that aren't due for three months.

'When you find out who your personal tutor is, don't get drunk – or make an idiot of yourself – if they are anywhere near your vicinity. They are the ones who are there to advise you, but they also write all your important references. In my experience, anything you say will be taken down as evidence! Try to make a good impression, but don't be fake.'
Ruth, 23, London

It's a good idea to think about what kind of student you want to be early on. Are you aiming for a First? Do you want a jam-packed schedule of extra-curricular activities alongside your studies? When are you going to do reading, writing, lab work, attend lectures, etc.?

At uni, your results will be much more reliant on yourself – there's no teacher looking over your shoulder to check that you've read every book on the reading list, but if you don't at least tackle half, your work will probably suffer. Tutors will help out – but with so many students on their books, they'll be much keener to help the ones that they can see are working hard and doing their best.

An empty timetable

If your timetable looks pretty blank at the start of term, fill it in yourself. It'll probably arrive with only your tutorials or lab sessions or classes, but fill it in with library sessions or research times and put them into your diary, so you can see that there is a lot to be done – you just have to organise it yourself. Don't only look at essay reading lists – follow up issues brought up in lectures, or lab sessions. If you come across something that you don't understand in a book, look it up to find out more.

If you're given two months to complete an assignment, that's because your tutor expects your work to take two months, not

TIP

'In your first year, just focus on the fun. To make the most of your fleeting time at uni, get involved in work and play – and since the work really kicks off in second and third years (or it should do if you want to use your degree for a job on the other side), save the slogging until then, and scrape by in the first year. Instead of working, prioritise joining clubs, attending socials and amassing mad memories of student silliness that will make your older eyes glow nostalgically and embarrass your kids! Don't forget to make good deep friends, too, who'll put up with your stresses and sporadic socialising in the working years.'
Tori, 20, Surrey

because they think that you've got a lot of *EastEnders* episodes to catch up on. (Well, not usually, anyway.) So start planning what you're going to do for the work immediately, break it down into chunks and organise your time.

Time management

After years slogging away at school, you might already know how you work best – but when the structured school day disappears and you're suddenly faced with weeks or months to complete assignments at uni, this can be worth re-thinking. Try recording a diary of when you work, how much work you get done and when you finish work. Then think about whether you work best under pressure, or prefer more of a long-distance marathon pace.

'I wish I'd known how much work there'd be at Oxford – there really is a lot more than my friends at other unis get, so you should be aware of that before applying.'
Joe, 19, Oxford

Next, look at when you work best. In my first two years I'd often work until 2 or 3 in the morning, and get up at 10, in time for a daily dose of Jeremy Kyle. But in my last year, as revision for finals drew nearer, I suddenly became an early bird, getting to the library by 6am (and leaving pretty early too), leaving evenings free to see friends and play tennis. Find your personal routine and work out when you're working most efficiently and cleverly. If you can read most intensively in the morning, arrange your timetable to do so. If you do prefer to work at night, switch off a bit before you go to bed – do something boring like organising your notes or do something fun like relaxing with friends, rather than moving right from your desk to your bed, because your brain will probably be too busy to sleep.

Motivation

Some people are self-motivated, do work as soon as it is set and smugly go out clubbing the day before essay deadlines, because they handed their work in two weeks beforehand. Other people require a time deadline to approach and a smack on the head before they feel motivated, so they finish work seconds before it's due. You'll probably already know what kind of learner you were at school – but at uni you might feel a bit more self-motivated. After all, you're there to study a topic that you chose to do, and you'll probably have a bit of leeway on assignments to focus on your favourite issues.

'Uni isn't like school; work ethics change, so don't be surprised if you have to find a whole new way of motivating yourself in order to do something that little bit constructive.'
Becca, 22, London

Still, there will probably also be times where you need a bit of help with motivation – a kick up the backside, let's call it – and while your tutors might have some advice, the only person who can really work on this is – you guessed it – you.

Procrastination: or wasting time...

Facebook, YouTube, clearing up your room, sorting out your pens to see which ones have the most ink – all these activities will have a sudden appeal when you're facing an essay deadline. (You'll find students like to dramatically call this an essay crisis – don't worry, this just means they haven't got round to writing it; world war has not broken out over a diplomatic problem in their last essay-writing session.)

Build up a routine which includes incentives. If work is due in on Thursday, for example, you might be tempted to muck around all day on Tuesday because you'll feel like there's loads of time. But if you organise something like a trip to the cinema on Tuesday night, you'll work harder during the day because you'll know that your busy diary means that you won't have time to waste.

Then make targets – tell yourself that you won't be able to go to the cinema until you've got to a certain stage in your lab work or essay research. Write your target(s) down in your diary or on a list. And stick to them.

Getting distracted

If you work in your room and find yourself wandering around looking for something to eat, or music to play, or answering phone calls, get out of your room and into a library. You'll feel less isolated, everyone else will be working, there will be more resources and fewer interruptions.

'Get uni work out of the way as soon as you are set it, before it starts to pile up. That way, you can enjoy other fun things at uni – there is so much to get involved with.'
Josh, 21, Manchester

Can't get started?

It's fine to have a routine that you like to perform before starting work, like arranging your pens in colour order or making a cup of tea… But when your routine takes longer than your actual working session, you need to have a re-think. Arrange to meet a friend at a certain time, and travel to the library or lab or faculty together. Break down your work into smaller chunks that are easier to face, make a list – and have an incentive (mine was a walk to the newsagent to buy a Cadbury's 'Dairy Milk') every time you tick something off.

Taking notes at lectures

Sometimes lectures don't deliver. Not many universities will admit that, but it's true. It can happen for two reasons. First, some lecturers are better than others, and the not-so-good lecturers are, well, dull. Not much you can do about this.

But if you're finding lectures tough because you're not being an active learner you can take action. I spent a long time assuming that by turning up at a lecture I'd soak in the knowledge, it would stay inside me for at least a few years, and I'd leave the lecture hall cleverer.

Well, it turns out that that's not true. 'Sit back and enjoy the ride' is not the best way to tackle a lecture. I discovered this when I started to revise for my first-year exams. I went to find my lecture notes and realised that on assorted weeks I hadn't

TIP

'When you get to uni you suddenly start meeting loads of different kinds of people and might not agree with everything that they believe in, but you can still get on with them – it's a good life skill… So keep in mind that many people can have different opinions on the same thing, but they can still all be right.'
Timothy, 22, Oxford

made them, couldn't understand them or couldn't read my own writing. If you have a serious problem listening to information while writing notes, consider asking the lecturer for permission to record the lecture on a Dictaphone, or most mobiles also have a voice recorder function.

Also be aware that most unis now always make lectures available in some format online – so there might be PowerPoint slides available on your subject's website, for example. Often this is password-protected and usually faculties organise training sessions to help you to work out how to access and best use the material made available online – if they do, attend! Spending an hour or so learning this once will save loads of time over the length of your degree, and re-visiting lectures online can also be really helpful when revision time rolls up. But it's even better if you get great notes from lectures in the first instance, so here are 10 steps for a perfect lecture-learning session.

TIP

'I'd advise that you actually go to lectures – I wish I had in first year – otherwise you get into a horrible routine that makes second and third years really hard to cope with – you have no idea what's hit you when it comes to working!'
Yael, 22, London

1. Think ahead

Imagine you're going out clubbing – you have to get yourself in the mood first. It's the same with a lecture. Before you arrive in the lecture theatre, think about the topic you're about to hear about – what ideas or theories are going to be discussed?

Read through last week's notes, or write your own notes on the topic. Organise yourself to arrive a few minutes early, and write down any questions that you'd like to have answered. If the answers don't crop up, you can be the keeno who asks the first question – always impresses tutors.

2. Bring the right tools

It's always annoying when you forget a pen and have to ask the guy next to you to borrow his stubby pencil. So check that you've got a couple of pens, a pad of paper, a highlighter and last week's lecture notes with you. A bottle of water can be nice too. And if you've got a few lectures during the day, check you have everything you need for a day's outing to the faculty – more paper and notes, a book to read in between – and prudent students will probably also include a bargainous packed lunch.

3. Use the handout

Most lecturers will provide a handout that will be waiting for you when you get to your seat. Read it – before the lecture starts, if possible – so you can see the quotes or information that you already have, and can annotate the sheet rather than trying to copy it out as the lecturer reads it.

4. Listen up

You might not want to be sitting in the front row, absorbing your lecturer's spraying spit, but don't sit at the back either – it'll be much more tempting to start texting a friend or catching up on your sleep. If you listen to the lecturer from the start, it'll be easier to stay alert and take it all in – it's like watching a TV show from the opening credits. And hey, it might even be interesting.

5. Focus on the important bits

You're not going to have time to write down everything that a lecturer says. So stick to the main points plus any references for follow-up work. Most lecturers outline their main points in an introduction and conclusion. Listen out for phrases like 'This lecture will…' or 'Then we'll look at…' or 'I'll outline…', then sit up like a very keen bean, and work out how to summarise your lecturer's key points.

6. Make your own code

You know how you always wanted to be a spy with a secret language? No? Oh – well, here's your chance anyway. Make shorter versions of the most common words and names in your academic vocabulary (e.g. if you studied linguistics, Ferdinand de Saussure might become 'Sau.', or a picture of a sausage, if you're the artistic type). You can also use common shorthand terms like

- ▶ 'pp.' for pages
- ▶ 'ch.' for chapter
- ▶ 'e.g.' – for example
- ▶ 'i.e.' – that is
- ▶ 'etc.' – and so on
- ▶ '+' – and
- ▶ '≠' – does not equal
- ▶ 'C18' – 18th century
- ▶ '∴' – therefore
- ▶ 'w/' – with
- ▶ '→' – leads to
- ▶ '←' – results from

I used quicker words like 'cld' instead of 'could', 'govt.' instead of government, 'b/c' for 'because' and '+ve' for positive. You can use abbreviations from text language too, and make your own symbols related to your subject area – but remember to keep them out of essays.

7. Organise your notes

Save time later on – if you incorporate things like bullet points and numbering in your lecture notes as you write them, they'll be much easier to follow (and learn from) later. Don't pack your notes into one squashy page – leave room between sections to add explanation or your own responses later. And file your notes in order of lectures, with their handouts filed too.

8. Make a shout out

Not literally – but if something has cropped up that you don't understand, either ask a question if the opportunity is offered, or go to the front to ask one-to-one – or, my personal favourite, email the lecturer afterwards. They're usually thrilled that someone cared enough about their lecture to bother to find out more, and they might offer to meet up to talk through it – if they do, that's where you start sneakily asking some questions related to your upcoming essay...

> **TIP**
>
> 'If like me you are people-shy, be aware that you will be in a lecture hall with a few hundred other people and not in a classroom with 30, like in high school – and that that will take mega getting used to! I still hate big lectures, but there are small classes too, which I prefer because you can ask questions more easily.'
> Paras, 22, London

9. Add to your notes immediately

Set aside 15 minutes after each lecture to sit down, read
through your notes, and add to them or make them clearer
– doing this while you still have the lecture in your head means
the notes will make more sense when you need them later to
write an essay or revise.

10. Discuss the lecture

Talk to coursemates about what they considered the key points
from the lecture – it will help you to understand them. I found
talking about work made it much easier to remember.

Resources

Here's a guide to tracking down books, plus top students'
website recommendations for a range of subjects.

*'Be nice to the library staff, a smile and being
polite goes a long way – and very often, fines and
renewals are down to their discretion... You'll be
surprised how much slack you'll be given for just
being nice to people.'*
Ruth, 23, London

How can a book cost £100?

Unfortunately academic books can cost more than a great night
out – and can be a lot less exciting. The library is obviously an
amazing alternative, but if there's a core textbook that you're
going to need a lot, it can be a worthwhile investment to buy it
– libraries will probably run out, anyway.

You don't have to buy brand-new books, though. Check out second-hand book shops (most university towns have quite a few), and their owners will often be happy to source books for you if they don't have them, plus make recommendations.

Another place to find cheap books is online. Use a book price-comparison site like www.bookbrain.co.uk to search for the cheapest price. Sites like Amazon marketplace and Abe Books (www.abebooks.co.uk) offer second-hand options.

Speak to graduating students about buying their copies (ask your faculty if they can help, or look on Facebook marketplace). But if you're going for a second-hand copy speak to your supervisor first to check whether there has been an updated reprint with required new information.

Academic websites

Whatever professors think of it, Wikipedia is a top student browsing option – although obviously you should be careful about double-checking things you read on it. But beyond Wikipedia – and even beyond Facebook – there are a load of academic gems online. Some sites require subscription, but most universities will hold membership, so ask your campus IT staff for log-in details.

Sites for all subjects

www.intute.ac.uk – created by seven UK unis, this site gives you academic links on a load of subjects, all recommended by subject specialists.

www.books.google.com – help build your reading list by searching for particular words or ideologies on this site, where you can search single books or across the whole (huge) book collection. I found it amazing for making bibliographies – whenever I forgot to write down where I'd read a quote, I'd search for it here to quickly track down the source. It even tells you the page number and gives you a screen-shot.

www.jstor.org – a massive archive of 1,000+ fully searchable journals, with academic articles on a huge range of subjects.

www.apple.com/education/itunesu – download lectures from tutors at places like UCL, Oxford, Cambridge and Dublin, plus foreign unis too. Listen to them on your iPod while out and about – never a wasted moment of learning!

Sites for humanities

http://plato.stanford.edu/ – this is a huge encyclopedia of philosophy. Each area of philosophy is updated and put together by a philosopher academic, so you can trust what you read.

www.sparknotes.com – few admit to using it, but I will! Sparknotes is a useful site for English students, providing plot summaries and thematic overviews of hundreds of literature texts. Of course, you have also read the actual texts. Probably…

www.quickmba.com – I'm told this site has loads of detail for economics, maths and management students, like the pros and cons of Porter's Five Forces. I'm not sure what that is, but I'm sure you are.

www.radstats.org.uk – find unusual stats on a wide range of subjects, from war to housing data, to jazz up a dull essay.

Science

www.ncbi.nlm.nih.gov/sites/entrez?db=books – another subscription-only site, this one works like an online library, offering the most-used undergraduate science reference works – so if a book has gone from the library shelf, go here.

www.nature.com/nature/index.html – *Nature* magazine's site gives daily updated biology info from journals.

www.sciencedirect.com/science/journal/01695347 – another way to access online journals, with the extra bonus of an RSS feed. Be really up to date – some of the articles here are published online first – so you could beat your tutors to the latest knowledge.

Law

www.justis.com – subscription legal library.

www.law-competitions.com – gateway to student law competitions around the world.

Media

www.theory.org.uk – this site is really easy to navigate. Written by a media professor, it includes essays and news plus video. The prof is so cool he even has a Facebook group…

www.aber.ac.uk/media/index.html – a gateway to online media studies resources.

Languages and linguistics

www.usingEnglish.com – do rapid text analysis here. The site can work out statistics on prose from counting numbers of unique words to calculating 'readability'.

www.bmlisieux.com – a big collection of French resources like literature, letters, journals and articles.

www.linred.com – a Spanish research journal with both English and Spanish articles.

Making notes from books and journals

If your notes are all over the place, it's time to get organised. Here are some note-making tips.

▶ Buy a folder to put your notes on a particular topic in, and every time you write notes on that topic, add them to a contents page at the front of your folder. You'll be able to quickly see what you've done so far and where to find it.

▶ Use abbreviations (see 'Taking notes at lectures' above).

▶ Find the important points by reading through your notes, then highlight them by underlining, or using capitals or a highlighter pen.

▶ Use different styles. Sometimes you just want linear notes written from a book. Other times, it can be helpful to do use a pattern, like a spider diagram or mind map. Play around to find out what works best for you.

▶ If you have a huge book to take notes from, consider sharing the task with a friend – but only if their notes are good enough for you to work from. If you're going to need to learn the book for exams, it's best to have your own notes.

▶ Use your own words to write notes, unless you're taking down quotes for an essay – in which case copy down phrases perfectly! Using your own words will help you to digest the ideas.

▶ Make each page of notes memorable in a different way – use pictures, diagrams, colour, Post-It notes, etc.

'Read things in books rather than photocopying them to read later. I spent hours photocopying books and articles in my second and third years and never read all of the stuff – it was a waste of time and money.'
Hannah, 21, London

Academic writing

Each subject will have its own nuances about style and, to make it even more complicated, usually universities and even individual tutors also have their own specifications about what they like to see in your academic writing. The best way to learn how to write is to do it, a lot. But there are certain 'rules' about style and tone and referencing that you'll need to learn about. Here are the main points.

What to write

Hope you didn't think you'd find a selection of here's-one-I-made-earlier – this isn't *Blue Peter*, y'know, and my essays took so long that I'd hate you to miss out on all the fun. But here is a guide to planning and writing essays.

Decoding titles

Essay titles can be confusing things. Here are some definitions of words that often crop up in essays.

▶ **Analyse, examine** – break your topic down, look at how the parts link up and judge their importance or merits.

▶ **Assess, explain, comment, describe, discuss** – give an account of what something means and consider its value. Imagine you are describing a topic to a friend (but use academic language).

▶ **Compare, contrast** – look at similarities and differences of two or more ideas.

▶ **Define, state** – write about the meaning of a topic or idea.

▶ **Evaluate** – describe the value (or success, or virtues, etc.) of a particular idea or concept (or its lack of value, if apt!).

▶ **Illustrate** – make your argument with the help of a range of examples.

▶ **Summarise** – write a condensed version of an idea, text, etc.

Carrying out research

Be imaginative when you plan your research – go beyond the core textbook and lecture notes. Start by writing a plan of where you're going to look, plus any book titles to track down, etc. Then look through as many books as possible to find relevant information; look at journals in libraries and online (see 'Academic websites' above), search magazines, newspapers, fieldwork, research notes, experiments, and ask coursemates what resources they are using.

'Always take a bottle of water to the library, and a secret stash of boiled sweets for energy. But keep them hidden from the library police...'
Mike, 21, Warwick

It's easy to get bogged down in research – it was usual to be unable to see the carpet in my uni room as it hibernated under piles of dirty plates, but at one point it was covered not in plates but hundreds of pages of printouts and photocopies and books. So don't try to cover everything ever written on your whole subject – develop skim-reading skills and don't get distracted by irrelevant chapters or information.

Make precise notes as you read; otherwise you'll have to go on a library treasure hunt (which is less fun than it sounds) to search for page numbers of quotes you've used after you've written your essay. So every time you start reading a book, write down its title, author, publisher, date of original publication, and the date of the edition you're reading. Then, every time you write down something found within the book, write the page number that you're reading from, and copy out the exact phrases to quote.

Make a plan

Once you've finished your main research, write another plan – this time looking at what you're going to write. Think about the main ideas you want to cover, write down the texts or material that will be 'core' to your essay, write down key quotes or examples and the order that you're going to incorporate them into your essay, and think about how your argument will develop. You'll probably want to do a few plans before coming up with a final 'master plan', with your points all ordered and leading up to your conclusion.

The introduction

Cracking the introduction isn't easy; but always keep in mind that unlike school essays, or creative writing, academic essays should include an outline of the whole essay's argument in the introduction.

I spent two years at uni writing essays that discussed possible arguments in the first few thousand words, before a great 'reveal' – like a *Stars in Your Eyes* special – of my 'real' argument in the last paragraph. In my final year, one of my tutors explained to me that this technique was a bit rubbish – and when I took his advice while writing my thesis, I soon realised it made sense.

Instead, you should outline your argument early on. You can phrase it with something like 'In this essay, I will show that…'. Strong introductory paragraphs that outline your basic argument are like putting on a great outfit before going on a date: they create a good first impression, so all you have to do is keep up that effort for the rest of the essay, and the marker will have fallen for your work – well, enough to get you a top mark, anyway.

Tone

Academic writing needs to have a tone that sounds individual (you are, after all, writing down your own unique response to a question or statement – or should be...) but is also quite formal. To sound serious and intelligent (and fit in with the accepted standards of academia), avoid a casual tone – so don't use too many rhetorical questions, and think about the 'register' of words you're using. A good way to do this is, before including a 'dodgy' word in an essay, think about whether you'd use it if you were talking to your most senior tutor. In reality, that means using terms like 'for example' rather than 'like', or 'narrative' rather than 'story'.

'Study hard and read widely. Failure is depressing.'
Jamie, 20, Nottingham

If you're worried that your essay tone is a bit too chatty or informal, reading can really help. Whatever subject you study, you're going to have a book list and lots of reading to be done. The texts on a reading list given to you by your tutor will probably all be written in a formal writing style – and the more you read, the more that style will become second nature.

Words to avoid

Avoid boring words like 'nice' or 'get' – there are usually much more accurate ones; for example, to replace 'nice' you could use 'beautiful' or 'useful', depending on the context. Use any specific words that you find in your course books to form an 'academic vocabulary' – a bank of new words relating to your subject which will have more relevant meanings to your essay context.

But don't get too highbrow. You've probably seen that forwarded email about spell checks ('I halve a spelling checker, it came with my pea see. It plainly marks four my revue mistakes I dew knot sea') – just as computer spell checks aren't faultless, it's also true to say that you shouldn't place all your trust in your computer's thesaurus. Just replacing a short word with a suggested longer one doesn't mean your work will sound better – do it too much and you'll sound pretentious; do it without thinking and the words might not even make sense.

Think about your reader – your tutor or supervisor will want to find writing that is clear and intelligent, not someone using long words for the sake of it. Writing should help you to communicate your ideas, not drown them.

Using quotations: referencing

If you use someone else's words or work, you have to acknowledge that use – otherwise you're guilty of plagiarism, and could face sinking into a pile of deep trouble, like being chucked off your course. So if you quote or paraphrase somebody else's ideas, or use someone else's research material or statistics, you should reference them in your work. Unis are really cracking down on plagiarism – pretending someone else's work is your own. They have top-notch software that can 'read' your work to check if any has been copied from someone else's writing. Penalties can include failure, re-sitting whole terms or even years, and even being thrown out of uni. So you need to make sure that you don't do it, even unintentionally. Whenever you read or research material, quote and take notes properly and then reference your work carefully – see below.

How do I include references?

Your subject handbook will have specific information on this. But here's a general guide.

There are lots of different ways to reference. At my uni, we could choose the system we used, as long as it was used consistently and accurately in each essay. I'd advise that you find one you like in your first year, and stick with it.

Referencing might seem boring, but many unis dock marks for poor referencing, so check your information more than once, and make sure everything – even the italics or underlining or font size you use – fits with the law laid down by your tutors.

Here's information on what to do using one common system – the Harvard system.

Harvard referencing system: author/date

Each time you refer to a piece of information that needs referencing, you write – within the passage, just after writing the quote or idea – and inside brackets, the author's surname, then date of edition you're using, then page number. Here's an example:

(Tobin, 2009: 70).

Then, you need to add this work to your bibliography or reference list, where you then put the detailed information. Here it would read: author's surname, author's initial followed by full stop, year of edition of work that you have used, title (underlined or in italics), place of publication, and publisher. Each part should separated by commas. Here's an example of how this book would be referenced in the bibliography:

Tobin, L., 2009, *The Guide to Uni Life,* London, Trotman.

All of your references are then arranged in alphabetical order of authors.

Referencing non-book material

If you're quoting or referring to some research that's not found within a book – maybe it's in a journal or newspaper, within your essay and in brackets, you again write the author's surname, then initials, then you add the year of publication of the journal, and page number. For example:

(Bloggs, J., 2009, p.1).

Then in the bibliography you would write the author of article's surname and initial, the date of journal, the article title in inverted commas, the journal title underlined or in italics, the journal's volume number, then issue number, then 'pp.' followed by the page numbers that the article begins and ends on. For example:

Bloggs, J., 2009, 'Article title here', *Journal title here,* no. 1, January 2009, pp. 1–29.

How to sound like an authority in your essays

Your tutor will probably have been working on their subject for decades, and will have a room full of every book written on the subject, ever. At least three of those bookshelves will probably be filled with books written by them on the topic. Even if your tutor is a relative newcomer to the academic scene, they'll definitely have a lot more experience than you – and so it can be difficult to know how to find something new to say. Likewise, in subjects where a side order of personal opinion alongside an essay's main course of fact can be acceptable (usually arts subjects), it can be hard to come up with a personal response when you're not aware of every single detail that's already been written or discussed.

The best way to get around this is to write your response fully but to also refer to any possible limitation or weakness that you can identify in your argument. So you can use phrases like 'For this essay the terms will be defined as…' or 'Within the scope of this essay, the argument will focus on the following implications…'. You can also refer to ideas or experts or texts that you know disagree with your argument, and then show why you think their disagreements are invalid.

Making sure that all your writing is backed up by examples (in science, that might be experiment results; in literature, a quote; in maths, a formula, etc.). This will help to ensure that your essay shows off your knowledge of the subject background.

Style

Unless you're writing a personal response, you should usually avoid first-person statements like 'I think' – they can be replaced with phrases like 'It could be said' or 'Arguably…' Essays are usually written in the third person ('it', 'they', etc.).

Write out full words like 'he is' rather than 'he's'. The same is true of phrases – instead of 'i.e.', write 'for instance' or 'for example'. Likewise, 'quotation' sounds better than 'quote'.

If you're using a word that can be abbreviated (like UCAS), write it out in full the first time you use it, and add the abbreviation in brackets afterwards, then for later references just use the abbreviation. So you might write, 'The process of entering further education is organised by the University and Colleges Admissions Service (UCAS)…', and then just use 'UCAS' for any further references.

Write in full sentences. Your paragraphs should usually be at least five or six sentences. Each paragraph should usually contain one point, fully made.

Check through all of your spelling and punctuation after you finish an essay. I found the best way to spot stupid mistakes was to slowly read the essay aloud.

Saving work

Dogs don't eat homework any more – but computers do. At my uni, they had a special policy that computer problems weren't acceptable reasons for late or missing work. So don't just save work on your computer, save it on memory sticks and CDs too. My favourite saving option was to email all my work to myself at the end of the day (Gmail accounts are best because they are free and have massive storage capacities) – so it was accessible even if I wasn't at my own laptop, and I knew it was saved somewhere far, far away from my room. Even if I didn't quite understand where or how it was saved in some distant area of cyberspace.

'It's a good investment to take your own printer to uni – they're cheap and if you have one in your room it'll come in handy for those annoying times when the library printer is out of ink or broken, and you have to hand in an essay in 3 minutes' time.'
Dan, 22, Cambridge

Bibliography and reference list

You might need one or both of these to end your work. A reference list names all the works quoted or referenced in your writing. A bibliography lists every work that you have read (even if you've only read parts of it), including ones not directly quoted but used to help you form ideas and opinions. See 'How do I include references?' above for more detail.

Essay contents check list

So now we've gone through what you should be thinking about including in your essays, here's a rundown to highlight the most important points. You might want to use this list as a check list to ensure that your first few essays fulfil all the necessary criteria.

▶ Introduction – does it concisely address the topic and outline your argument?

▶ Structure – have you planned your essay? Does each paragraph develop your argument towards a solid conclusion?

▶ Sentences – are any too long? A good way to check is reading aloud – if you need to pause mid-sentence to catch your breath, it's too long.

▶ Paragraphs – are they long enough to address a point coherently? Does each one connect to the next? Avoid repeatedly starting paragraphs with the same word. Especially if it is 'therefore'.

▶ Spelling and punctuation – have you checked for mistakes?

▶ Style – have you avoided slang, and written phrases and abbreviations in full? Have you followed the department's advice about the fonts, spacing, printing format, etc.?

▶ Name – have you written your name and/or candidate number on each page? Have you included page numbers and stapled pages together?

▶ Word count – is the essay the right length?

▶ Conclusion – do you finish in a concise and coherent way, and avoid summarising your earlier points?

▶ References – have you written your references and headers/footnotes accurately and in an academic and consistent style?

▶ Bibliography – have you completed this accurately and in an academic and constant style?

▶ Plagiarism – is there a plagiarism certificate to sign? Have you avoided inadvertent plagiarism?

Feedback

If you get a bad mark for an essay, especially one you took a long time over, it can be tempting to rip it up and shove it in the bin. Bad idea – if you don't find out why you did badly, it'll be hard to improve for your next piece of work. Read your tutor's comments. If you think your tutor has misunderstood your work, or you can't understand where you went wrong, ask for more feedback, either in a face-to-face meeting or through a note or email. Ask how the essay could be improved, and for practical steps that will help you do better next time.

A special note on science work

Scientists often think arts students are a bit of a joke. I have lost count of the number of times a scientist has mocked me because, while their working day starts at 9am, I'd still be slumbering. But I just can't see why an early start is a good thing worth boasting about. And, for the record, studying English is not a doss subject…

TIP

'If you study science (like me), pick your lab partner with care! Go for the cleverest, nerdiest person you can find – in the lab you're not there to chat about last night's gossip but to find decent results, so the better your partner, the better your grades.'
Katrina, 22, London

Anyway, I'm magnanimously overlooking all the sarky comments and have enlisted my clever scientist friend Katrina, currently doing a science Masters at Oxford, to explain all about how to hit high scores in scientific research and labs. Hold tight… it's over to Katrina.

Deciphering a scientific research paper

Your average science paper will be divided into the following sections.

▶ An Abstract – a short paragraph on the front page summarising the main aims and conclusions of the paper. You can usually spot it from ten feet away – it'll be the bit in bold or boxed in. To avoid wasting time, read this paragraph first to check that the paper is relevant for what you're after. Then re-read it after you have finished the paper – it'll help draw together the main points.

▶ An Introduction – a few paragraphs detailing the background knowledge of the themes to be discussed in the paper.

▶ Material and Methods – this bit is usually cowering away in a smaller font, found either before/after Results, or at the end of the paper. It gives an account of the practical techniques used. Unless you are particularly interested in methods, you can bypass this section.

▶ Results – often divided into distinct paragraphs with their own subheading describing the main findings. Results can sometimes be very detailed and complicated, so read the Discussion section first, then go back to the relevant paragraph in Results if you need more info.

▶ Discussion – the main bulk of the paper, this bit includes explanation and analysis of results, providing scientific meaning and relevance. Sometimes beneficial to read this section before Results – the explanation makes the results easier to understand.

▶ Conclusion – some papers, but not all, bring together the main findings into a concluding paragraph. Look back at the Abstract after reading the Conclusion to confirm the paper's main points.

So – I reckon this is the best order to read a scientific paper: Abstract – Introduction – Discussion – (Results) – Conclusion – (Methods)

Referencing a science paper

People reference scientific papers in a few different ways. I'd recommend the following format for its clarity:

Name of authors (in the order given in the paper); title of the paper; the journal it was written in and the year; volume: page numbers.

And here's an example I made earlier:

M. J. Valstar, G. J. G Ruijter, O. P. van Diggelen, B. J. Poorthuis, F.A. Wijburg, 'Sanfilippo syndrome: A mini-review', *J Inherit Metab Dis*, 2008, 31: 240–252.

(Thanks, Katrina.)

Writing a dissertation

An undergraduate dissertation (sometimes called a thesis) is a long essay, usually between 5,000 and 20,000 words, that addresses a particular topic or question. Apart from the word length, what people sometimes freak out about is the fact that dissertations usually count towards their final degree mark. That's not always true – you should check with your department, but you'll probably work it out anyway because if your dissertations 'counts', then your friends will probably suddenly decide to drop their social life to focus on work until DD Day – dissertation deadline.

Departments will usually provide a handbook or give a lecture on what they expect from students' dissertations. Since your department's guidelines will be specific to your course, and are probably written by the people who'll be marking your work, follow these to the letter.

More generally, you should follow all the usual essay conventions, but there are some extra ones too. So here is a look at expectations and features of dissertations – and hopefully by the end it won't seem so scary after all.

'Always have some snacks in your room for long days and nights spent inside during essay crises. Dried food is good, as it keeps longer – dried fruits, crisps, rice cakes, biscuits are all ideal.'
Francis, 22, Nottingham

Structure

Giving your dissertation structure can be crucial. By deciding on a structure, including a title, general contents list, a plan of the topics you're going to address and a reading list, you'll have broken down a huge task into lots of smaller ones that are easier to tackle. Secondly, a good structure – one that shapes the dissertation into a strong, developed argument – can make the difference between a good mark and a great one.

The best way to make sure your work is well structured is to plan both your work and your time well in advance. Use your diary to create a set of deadlines leading up to a completion date about a week before the final deadline, leaving you lots of time to check through your work.

Start as early as possible – that doesn't necessarily mean you'll finish early (I nerdishly started my thesis on the first possible day, and finished my obsessive checking through at 2am on the day it was supposed to be handed in) – but it will help you feel more relaxed about your work. Starting early will also give you a head-start on getting books at the library and talking to tutors, which is especially important if lots of students are looking at similar topics at the same time.

Once you've finished most of your reading and research, come up with an 'abstract' – a few paragraphs summarising the contents of your dissertation and its findings or conclusion. Sometimes this will be required as part of your dissertation submission, but even if it is not, it's useful to help you to start work, even though you might adapt it before handing in your work.

You might also need a material or literature review – this is a summary of the current literature/experiments/etc. currently available on your topic of study. It helps you to make sure that you're not repeating someone else's work and can give you an idea about undiscovered areas to look into. You might have to raid the library shelves, or find out about scientific experiments, or something completely different. You're going to want to show off all that research, and that's what a 'literature review' in your dissertation will do, but don't make it so detailed that it dwarfs your own work. Include the seminal tomes on the topic as well as the most up-to-date theories. Keep careful note so you can include them in your bibliography (see above). Think of the dissertation as a unique opportunity to explore your own interests – when else are you going to have this much time to discover new ideas, and eat loads of chocolate whilst doing it?

Studying abroad

As you rush to duck inside a lecture hall to avoid pouring rain or snow or wind or the generally rubbish British winter, the idea of spending a term or a year studying abroad might sound tempting. It tempts thousands of students every year – in fact, last year 10,000 signed up to the Erasmus scheme, spending time studying in Europe, while more studied in countries like the USA and Canada and the Far East. There are huge benefits, and all of my friends who spent time studying abroad came back raving about the experience. Actually, sometimes they go on for a little too long about Octobers spent strolling around in T-shirts and no-pressure exams. But anyway, here's a look at the whos, hows, whats and whys about studying abroad.

'I wish I'd known more about the opportunities to study abroad when I started uni – there are so many chances, and there are amazing options, so I'd recommend freshers start researching them as soon as possible.'
Sarah, 22, Nottingham

What's the point?

If you've ever wanted to try out living overseas, now – when you've got few responsibilities and your brain is still young enough to rapidly absorb a new language and culture – is a good time to do it. You'll probably be totally petrified by the idea of 'starting again' with a new uni life far from home, but that can also be a life-changing experience.

Many schemes will also mean you can benefit financially – from lower or cancelled tuition fees. Long-term, having more maturity and confidence and experience of another culture (especially if you've learnt the language), picked up from a year abroad, could be even better financial news – your experience will mean bonus CV points, which could mean a better job and higher salary. Some year abroad visits may give you credits towards your course; others may be an opportunity to enjoy academia without assessments.

How to sort out a year abroad

Not all unis offer years abroad – and some only offer the opportunity to linguists – but most do. Find out more by contacting your tutor to see whether your uni participates in study abroad schemes or exchanges. Within Europe, one of the easiest ways to organise a period of study abroad is through the Erasmus scheme, organised through the European Union. You can look for universities and courses that are involved in the scheme at www.britishcouncil.org/erasmus, by calling 029 2039 7405 or emailing Erasmus@britishcouncil.org

Worldwide university exchanges, to countries like North America, Australia or China, are also available at many universities. Some even have campuses abroad – Nottingham University, for example, has campuses in Malaysia and China as well as other year abroad options that UK students can attend for a term or more. Bear in mind that some study abroad

TIP

'Studying abroad is an amazing adventure, but think carefully about where and when you go – and think really hard about the cost of living. If you cannot afford Norwegian prices, don't spend six months there. If you do go to Norway (like I did), go during the summer, when it's warm and light and people spend time outside.'
James, 20, Nottingham

options are over-subscribed and you may have to choose a few alternative destinations and see which you are allocated; sometimes preferences are decided by your exam grades or other academic achievements.

Before you confirm attendance on a year abroad scheme, you should have written confirmation from your UK uni about how it will ensure that the foreign uni supports your studies. You should also be clear on issues like how much work the uni expects you to do in a different language, if relevant. You should also ask your tutor what happens if you fail a year abroad, and what impact that could have on your degree.

The year abroad experience

This is something I missed out on (it was never likely when I applied to study English, I guess...), but I lived it vicariously through long Skype sessions with friends who were studying abroad. Here, Howard – who recently spent an Erasmus year in Valencia, Spain, as part of his degree in economics – gives his top tips and experiences.

Howard's story

My year abroad was the most enjoyable time of my degree – I met new people, lived next to the beach and developed my language skills. But that's not to say it was all straightforward. Finding a place to live turned out to be an especially stressful experience. I'd only been in the country a few hours when I had to start flat-hunting, there was limited availability and I didn't understand the Spanish system. But I ended up renting a room in a flat with local students – and I'm so glad I did. The best way to learn the language is to live with locals. My flatmates introduced me to their friends, explained local customs and told me about cool events; even when we were just relaxing at the flat in front of the TV, I was improving my language as well as having a good time.

The process of finding somewhere to live will vary depending on where you are – some universities offer rooms in halls to foreign students, but lots don't. I'd recommend talking to students who've studied in the place that you're going – they can tell you the studenty areas and the best way to sort it out without being ripped off. It's worth spending some time doing research – accommodation is one of the most important things. If you're living in the wrong place, far from campus or from the areas where everyone socialises, then it can put a downer on the whole year.

Living abroad has some amazing opportunities, but don't expect to be having fun all the time. I missed my family, friends and my girlfriend. At the start, when I didn't have internet or a phone, I felt pretty isolated. But that's another advantage of living with local people – they're used to all the administrative stuff, and know the best companies and so on.

It's easy to forget about the actual studying that you've got to do when abroad – at the beginning I didn't understand a lot of the lectures; it was really hard to take notes and understand the language at the same time. But as I started to settle down and improve my language skills, I was surprised how quickly it became second nature.

Other things to bear in mind are to do with your finances – check out whether it would be cheaper to open a local account or stick with your British one. Also, make sure you budget for the whole year, and be aware of the exchange rate – and what everything costs in pounds. Find out the average price of things like electricity before you get the first bill, so you can work out how much to put aside.

Most foreign universities will insist on you having travel insurance. You should shop around to get the best value, but make sure you pay enough to get everything you need, and don't have too large an excess. You'll normally need a special policy that allows you to be away for a long period of time – standard holiday insurance policies don't usually cover this. You might not want to shell out on an expensive policy, but anything can happen and it's a lot scarier when you're miles from home and family. Someone I knew fell off a second-floor balcony and broke both his arms, and insurance is so important at times like that. Also, if you're studying in the EU, apply for a (free) European Health Insurance Card.

Note that you might need a visa if you're studying in certain countries, so check with the country's embassy; if you do, your UK university will probably be able to advise.

Finally – expect to have some kind of culture shock. Be prepared for different eating habits and timings. Early in my stay, I was ready to go out clubbing about nine o'clock, when my flatmates told me they normally headed out about midnight! Try to be as open-minded as possible – and have a great time.

Chapter 7

Exams

Exams suck – we all know that. I looked forward to my eighteen hours of Finals with about as much excitement as an arachnophobic feels about the prospect of getting into a bath full of tarantulas. I was especially apprehensive about approaching these degree-deciding exams as, despite working hard for my first year exams, I did pretty badly in them. I think the reason for that was that I'd prepared for them a bit like A Levels – learning lots of prepared answers, and delivering them off pat wherever seemed prudent. That approach turned out to do me no favours, but luckily the first year exams hadn't counted towards my degree, and by the time Finals rolled around I'd got used to uni exams.

Since pretty much all of us have to do them, it's best to get on with the revision and spend less time moaning about them. So here are some tips to face exams head on and win. Oh yes – it's time for fighting talk.

Make a revision timetable

When you think about it, exams aren't that different from any other kind of learning you do at uni – so, just as it's a good idea to be organised when you're facing an essay deadline, the same is true of exams. Make a revision timetable as early as possible so you can spread out your revision – but obviously don't start so far in advance that you can't remember anything. Timings will differ for everyone, but for my Finals – which started in mid-May, counted for almost all of my degree and took place in the space of a week – I started revising at the end of March.

At some unis, not all exam papers are worth the same number of points – so make sure you know how important a paper is when you're deciding how much time to spend revising for it.

By exam time, you should know how long you can keep working on something at peak – for me, it was about an hour, so I scheduled my timetable to work for hour-long blocks, then arranged to eat a meal, or meet a friend, or do errands. Organise your timetable around group learning activities – so if your tutor has set you a mock exam on DNA structures, schedule DNA revision in the days leading up to that mock exam.

'I would have appreciated knowing what other students thought was a normal social life while at uni – I felt there was too much emphasis on partying, to the detriment of my studies, and regret that balance.'
Simon, 25, Manchester

And think about whether you prefer to alternate between topics to avoid boredom, or to get whole topics done in the same time – take all these issues on board when making your timetable. Don't go crazy about how long you can revise for – even if you can stay sitting at a desk for hours on end, you won't be taking as much in towards the end of a session, so take lots of short breaks.

You should also do some group study to prevent your revision getting too solitary – your tutor might arrange group study sessions, but, if not, do it together with your classmates. Decide on some topics you want to go through, and bring notes or questions or books to discuss together.

Don't give up your normal activities

When exams are looming it can seem necessary to dump everything apart from study – but that's not a good plan. Big boozing nights should probably be avoided close to exams, but the odd trip to a restaurant or an evening spent watching DVDs with friends can help you to work better.

Build some exercise into your schedule too – swimming, jogging, the gym or group exercise can help you to feel better and improve your concentration. Shove some exercise into your routine at a time you're not working well – if, for example, you find it hard to get going in the late afternoon session, go for a run before blitzing a revision session in the evening.

But, while you're mostly sticking to your normal routine, I reckon exam time means it's OK to drop some activities – I wouldn't bother hoovering if I was rushing around revising, for example. Some things can just wait!

Boost your energy through your diet too – obviously it's totally acceptable to eat yummy snacks, but eat healthy meals too – keep up a balanced diet of fruit and veg, proteins and carbs, plus brain food like oily fish. I absolutely hate fish and never eat it, but a few weeks before exams I read about the brainy benefits of fish and forced down a couple tins of tuna. I think this best proves how crazy and superstitious I got before exam time, rather than the idea that those two cans of tuna paved the way to academic success, but still… Eat well; it's good for you and your exam grades.

Lots of people rely on drinks like 'Red Bull' and coffee to get through exams – when I got into the habit of being in the library early, I started drinking coffee for the first time in my life. Coffee and other caffeine drinks do help you to feel more alert, and improve concentration. Just don't drink too much. I started drinking energy drinks in the evenings after exams to help me to cram for the next day, but found I couldn't sleep by night time, so just stuck to morning cups of coffee. Avoid caffeine tablets too, if possible – they can make you 'buzz' a little too much, and can bring on sleeping problems.

Stop revising a good hour before you go to bed – spend that time relaxing with friends or watching TV or a DVD, or listening to music or reading a (non-course) book. To help you sleep, it can help to have a mug of warm milk, and a bath or shower.

Find your best revision style

Sitting in a silent library writing revision notes doesn't work for everyone – and no one should do the same kind of revision all the time, because it will rapidly get very boring. Make your revision active – through note-taking (see below) and by breaking it up with other learning activities. For example, consider going to the odd lecture for revision. My Finals exam included two years' worth of material, so the lectures that I'd attended (and sometimes not attended) during second year were running again for the current second year students. Attending these lectures can be a quick way to re-cap something I'd last heard a year before – and, honestly, some lecturers really do deliver their content, word-for-word, the same year after year.

Making notes

Most students start revision by making notes – but don't stick to one source: if you're spending weeks taking notes from the same book, your notes will be one-sided and your brain will be bored.

▶ Use different books, plus your essays, lecture notes, tutorial notes, journals, newspapers, reputable websites, magazines, research reports, and new academic findings.

▶ Find sources that help you look at the subjects you need to cover in your revision in a new way. Adding some really up-to-date information to your notes (the kind you'll pick up from a really recent journal, for example) will also impress examiners who are having to sit marking many, many papers which will often all use similar arguments and sources. But, just because you've found a really new idea or quote, think before you write it all down. Will it be relevant to your exams?

▶ Don't learn massive chunks of quotations off by heart; have a few key phrases in your notes – you want to have quotes that support your argument rather than paraphrase someone else's. Once you've 'finished' (or done enough) of a particular topic, condense your notes into abridged versions. I kept doing this over and over again until I had index cards with just a few key terms to jog my memory. Every time you re-write the content will help you to remember it.

▶ Just as you're not sticking to one source to make your notes, write your notes in different ways. Some might benefit from a spider diagram; others could be made into pictures.

▶ Use different coloured pens if that helps – or different coloured papers: one of my uni friends had read that things written on yellow paper are easier to remember, so he bought a chunk of that for his revision notes. He got a First, so it might be a good idea...

Memory tips

Repetition is one of the best ways to memorise things – repeat facts out loud, write them again and again, use flashcards and visual triggers, like drawing pictures from your notes and putting them up on the wall (I put mine in front of a mirror). It's a good idea to download relevant podcasts from iTunesU, where ideas might be phrased in new ways.

The smell of cinnamon and peppermint are also thought to boost alertness (so you could try gum). Rosemary is supposed to boost memory, so one of my friends at uni bought a rosemary plant during revision – but then we found another piece of research that said that rosemary boosts long-term memory but can make recall slower – so she relocated the plant into the corridor… Recall vs memory – up to you to decide which is more important!

Past papers

Track down past exam papers (they're usually available online to print off, as well as on file in faculty libraries) to see the format of your questions. Looking at lots of papers – say, those from the past five years – will help you to see any trends in questions. I went through each paper, picked out the main themes that kept being asked, then typed out the questions that were asked on those themes in the past five years to see what I should be looking at.

As your revision develops, you'll want to start tackling some past papers. Make essay plans rather than writing out endless practice essays, but do complete some timed practice papers – you'll probably quickly realise that you can't fit in all the points that you want to, and will have to be selective.

On the day

Make sure you have checked where your exam is and leave plenty of time to arrive early. Check your bag before you leave to ensure you've got all the necessary materials, but don't take extra things like your mobile, since you won't be able to take it into the exam hall and it's safer to leave it at home.

Try to eat a good breakfast – with not too many drinks; you don't want to waste time on toilet trips… You might want to go through your material one more time before heading off to the exam – this will probably make you feel more reassured.

In the exam

▶ Most uni exams will give you choices about which questions to answer. If this is the case, read through the whole paper before making your decision.

▶ If you're writing a long answer worth a lot of marks, write a plan for the first question you're going to tackle. I had to answer three essay questions, and my tutor advised me to first answer a question I felt the most confident about, then answer my weakest question, then answer my second strongest at the end. Leaving the weakest to the end will just make you panic.

▶ If you're worried about remembering facts or formula or other memorised things, write them down on your exam question paper (if you're allowed to write on it) as soon as the exam begins, so you can then focus on answering the questions and they're there for your reference if you need them.

▶ Read all of your instructions and questions carefully.

▶ Check whether any questions are compulsory or optional.

▶ Work out how you're going to time your progress through the question paper – split up your time according to how many marks are attributed to particular answers.

▶ Allow time for planning – and write a quick plan for you to refer to as you answer the question to avoid going off a track. If you have an hour to answer an essay question, spend at least ten minutes planning your response.

▶ Think about what the question is actually asking of you – just because it mentions the word 'America' doesn't mean that you should produce the perfect answer on the American perception of progress that you learnt off by heart last night – the question could be looking at something completely different, while another question might focus on progress without mentioning America – so underline the key words or phrases in the question, and think hard about what questions you choose to answer and what to include in your answer.

▶ Don't write everything you know on a topic – be selective.

▶ Show off to the examiner throughout that you are answering the question – go back and read it at the beginning of every new paragraph...

▶ But don't keep writing 'and so this shows...' followed by the essay question. Just summarise in your introduction how you will be shaping your argument to answer the question.

▶ Under exam conditions you will probably be making one point per paragraph. Use your conclusion to bring your earlier arguments together to hammer home your response to the question.

If you're freaking out...

If you do feel a rising sense of panic – like I did in the first of my Finals, when I turned over the exam paper and found that the usual three pages of questions had been whittled down to just one page and I couldn't answer a single one – take a few deep, slow breaths. If you like, tell yourself (in your head) something like 'This is going to be OK, I've revised and am ready'.

If your mind goes blank, try to relax, put down your pen, and take a deep breath. Think about something else for a few seconds, then read over what you have written so far. If you still can't remember what you were writing, leave a few lines to come back to that sentence, start a new point and then return to fill the gap before finishing the essay.

If you find yourself running out of time, try to speed up your handwriting, but don't panic. Answer all remaining questions as succinctly as possible, splitting up your left-over time on the outstanding questions. If you really don't have enough time to finish a question, it might be worth listing your remaining points in bullet point form – you might not get extra marks, but sometimes you do, so it's worth a try. Don't waste time writing an excuse to the examiner about why you haven't finished – just concentrate on getting closer to 'finished'.

TIP

'Don't work too hard... One night near my Finals, I awoke with a strange sense of being in the wrong place. After many minutes of bleary blinking I realised I was in the library with pages of "asdffffffff" typed out in the middle of my essay on my laptop, and a strange coat over my shoulders. Next morning I discovered it was the security guard's coat. He had taken pity after watching me falling asleep for several hours through his shift. I think another moral of this story is to always be nice to the maintenance crew!'
Tori, 21, Oxford

What not to write...

Just as essays shouldn't contain slang or abbreviations, the same is true of exams. Don't let your time constraints affect your academic writing style – retain the high register you've developed throughout your essays or tutorial work, and avoid first-person statements like , 'I think…'. Instead use phrases like 'This essay will show…', to propose strong arguments supported by evidence.

Don't try to cram something into your essay (or 'download' a pre-learnt essay) just because it got a good mark at some earlier date – if a point is not relevant to the exam question, it will not help your mark, no matter how good a point it is – and too much irrelevant material can lead to you losing marks.

After the exam

Tempting as it will seem, don't launch into a massive post-mortem session (especially not with the class genius), because it'll just make you panic. Other students' exam experiences won't be the same as yours – but that doesn't mean yours went badly. If you really need to talk to someone about the exam, contact your tutor. But try to forget about the exam, if possible, and have a break to relax before focusing on the next one.

If you had any problems in the exam, like health concerns or you had received news right before the paper that affected your ability, tell an invigilator in the exam hall. He or she will take steps so that examiners know to take your situation into consideration, if appropriate.

Exam stress

Much like normal stress (see Chapter 4, 'Health'), a bit of this can make you work harder – but if it starts to get out of control, or you're feeling ill or unable to sleep or concentrate for long periods of time, find someone to talk to, like your personal tutor, or a doctor, or visit a counsellor on campus – all will be able to help.

Try to keep a sense of perspective – the exams might seem like the most important thing ever right now, but once upon a time, didn't GCSEs feel like just the same thing? And no one cares about them now! Remember that exams are just one part of your uni career – and all you can give them is your best shot.

Chapter 8

Righting wrongs

Sometimes, despite the best of intentions, things at uni can go wrong. Maybe your course isn't what you thought it would be, or your university experience isn't offering the opportunities you'd hoped for. Or the course is just too hard and you've failed important exams. If one of these things happens to you, keep in mind that university is just as important for its modules in the degree in Life Experiences – like how to cook a meal – as courses on the ambiguities within Eliot's 'The Waste Land', or how fission occurs in prokaryotic cells.

So take a step back and don't rush into decisions. This chapter looks at possible problems you might be facing, and practical steps to take to improve your situation or, if necessary, extract yourself from somewhere you don't want to be. There's also advice on the best people to approach if you've changed your mind about one of the big factors in your student life.

The possible problems

Wrong university

You don't like the location, people, staff, or have another reason to want to Get Out Of There Fast. Make sure you've given yourself at least a few weeks to get 'into' uni life – settling in can take time. Even if you're certain that you want to move, seek advice before doing anything drastic. See below for more details.

Wrong point in your life

You or someone close to you has problems that mean you can't focus on uni life and studies. Or your finances are in such a mess that you need to take some time out to earn more pennies. You may want to think about deferring for a year, or more, then returning. Again, seek advice about your options – a year with a job could solve the problem if it's financial. Even if you're sure you want to quit uni for ever, or you land a dream job that puts you off studying for life, defer rather than withdraw if possible – it keeps your options open.

Wrong accommodation

You've tried really hard but just can't get on with your housemates, or the actual house or flat just doesn't cut the mustard. Speak to your accommodation organiser as soon as possible and explain why you are unhappy. This problem will probably be easier to fix if you're in halls, but if there's a serious fault with private property you can still rectify the problem. If you don't know what to do, contact your Students' Union housing advisor.

Failed the year

First, try not to panic. Take a few days to think about what went wrong and what you want to do next, and find out as much advice as possible. Organise a time to meet with your tutor or a member of the faculty. Your options will depend on the reason for failure – ill health, for example, may mean you are granted special dispensation to continue without re-sitting, but this will greatly depend on individual circumstances.

Make sure you seek advice from as many sources as possible, including your course tutors, your subject admissions tutors, your Students' Union representative, other students who have been or are in your situation, and your parents.

If the reasons you failed are easily solved – you did not work hard enough, for example, and you can prove that you would remedy this situation, you will have to convince tutors that you would work harder and will probably have to re-sit examinations.

Note that the rules on re-sitting examinations will vary at different universities, and will be very different for students on professional courses like medicine or teaching – discuss your specific options with your own academic advisors. If you fail a summer exam, you'll normally have the opportunity to re-sit in August – so think in advance about the practical implications: you may have to find accommodation the night before the exam, for example.

If, however, there is a more serious problem, such as you found the course too difficult even with extra academic help, or misunderstood the nature of the course, or do not want to re-sit or continue the course, then you will have to re-consider your options, which may include applying to another course or university, or perhaps having some time out.

Wrong course

Nothing about your course is what you expected, you have no enthusiasm to turn up to work, you don't get on with your tutors. If you think changing courses will solve your problems, consider doing so. First discuss your ideas with a tutor and someone from the careers service, who will help you to look at your options. Doing so – especially if you have written proof of serious consideration and improved prospects with a new course – will help your bid to ensure your uni funding is transferred when you do so.

> **TIP**
>
> 'Think – really, really hard – about whether you'll actually enjoy the course that you're applying for. I know it is hard without actually doing the course, but reading up on the course synopsis will be beneficial – I didn't do that when I applied for maths, and after I got to uni I realised that I absolutely hated it. I ended up having to keep changing courses (maths to engineering, to natural sciences and finally settling with geophysics) – because I think life is too short to do something you don't like – so take time and do something that you get pleasure from.'
> Paras, 22, London

Course complaints

If you want to stay on your course but are annoyed with the quality of teaching, or unfair marking, or a lack of feedback, you can make a complaint. Universities have their own processes for student complaints, which might include you contacting a course rep, someone who is supposed to represent the student view on courses. Otherwise, ask your Students' Union about what to do about your complaint and what kinds of appeal processes exist at your uni. Ensure you have adequate evidence, and see if other students have also experienced your grievance.

If internal methods fail to solve or address your problem, you can make a complaint to the Office of the Independent Adjudicator for Higher Education, a free, independent student complaints scheme. Find out more at www.oiahe.org.uk or call 0118 959 9813.

Steps to take before you decide to leave your course

► First of all, keep attending lectures and don't quit doing your work. You'll either decide to stay on your course, and need that work, or decide to change, and need a tutor reference – so keep ploughing on.

► If money problems are your biggest issue, ask your uni about bursaries, grants, scholarships – anything going in Chapter 2.

► Discuss your concerns and decisions – see 'Who to go to for advice', below. Don't officially withdraw from your course until you have spoken to a careers advisor and tutor about your options.

► Consider adapting your course – see whether you can switch modules within your course, or change from joint honours to single honours, or move around your main and minor subjects.

► Check availability – if you're keen to start a new course, ensure it has places available. This may affect your funding options, too.

► Check out your debts – find out if you'll have to repay any debts from student loans or overdrafts when your student status changes. Speak to your local authority, or the Student Loans Company, and the bank about your new status. Also check if you have to pay out penalties for leaving your accommodation early.

▶ Find out if you're entitled to any study credits – these can be used for future study, so speak to your personal tutor, or someone from your faculty, about academic credits. But check how long any credits would remain valid – nursing course credits, for example, have 'sell-by dates' – so do your research.

Changing courses

You will first need to speak to the head of admissions in charge of your preferred (new) course to see if you are able to have a place on the course. Next, contact your local authority (or the Student Loans Company, if your cash came from them in the first place) for permission to start a course in another academic year, since they are footing a large chunk of the bill for your education. It's best to sort out these two factors before asking your current department to withdraw your registration from their course.

Be aware that leaving a course early can affect your entitlement to future financial support. So speak to your local authority or the Student Loans Company about this first, and discuss your options with a student finance expert at your uni.

Next up are more practical steps: Start by asking your student financers for a 'change of circumstances form'. You can download this from the Student Finance England site, www.direct.gov.uk/studentfinance. You'll also find downloadable forms on the site that allow you to apply for a 'tuition fee loan request' to cover any cost differences if your new course fees are higher.

If your (potential) new uni approves you for its course, it will send your funding authority a 'Notification of Student Transfer' form and they will reassess your funding options. Be aware that if you start a new course part-way through, you'll probably have to work hard to catch up, and may have to attend revision sessions or extra lectures.

Who to go to for advice

Ultimately your decision to change something about your uni life – be it your course or institution – should be made by your own judgement, but advice will help you to make up your mind. Speak to friends and family who have been in the same position. Or, for less partial advice, especially if you're concerned about the kind of degree you'll need for future careers, head to your university careers service and book a one-to-one session with an advisor.

If you're under 19, in England and Wales you could also call Connexions (080 800 13219, www.connexions-direct.com), a government-funded career guidance service. In Scotland, you could speak to Careers Scotland (0845 8 502 502, www.careers-scotland.org.uk). Or look on graduate careers websites like Prospects (www.prospects.ac.uk) for more information.

Your personal tutor will normally have had experience of dealing with students with problems with their course or uni life. Speak to him or her about any worries that are affecting you. Make sure there's time for a proper chat – don't try to catch your tutor after a lecture; email him or her, outlining your situation, and ask to book an appointment. If you're struggling but enjoying a course, your tutor may be able to organise study skills or tutorial support or suggest similar course options at your uni. If you're certain that you want to change, they may be able to help out if they have colleagues at other universities. Try to get your tutor on board early – he or she will often be a very useful source of help. If you need more emotional support, pay a visit to your university counselling service.

Even if it seems like changing courses is too expensive or too much hassle or you just feel very confused, keep in mind that hundreds of students switch classes or courses or degrees or institutions every year, and end up much happier. An example is Imogen, who studied illustration at Loughborough University.

Imogen's story

Before I started my degree at Loughborough, I spent a year at Sussex University studying English. The course wasn't what I'd expected, and eventually I decided to leave. At the time, it was such a hard choice to make, I didn't want to let people down. But looking back, it was the right choice. And when I first moved into halls at Loughborough I met a girl who was going through the same situation, so I was in a good position to offer advice. She managed to change courses, and the experience meant we became very close friends – that was just one of the good things that came out of changing universities.

A unique experience ...

One of my uni housemates – who graduated with me last year – called me a few weeks ago to tell me she had just spent three hours reading through her dissertation folder and all its essays and notes. Until four in the morning. It wasn't the academic stuff she wanted to re-cap – she'd just suddenly missed everything about uni life, and all those scrawling notes had brought it all back.

I knew exactly how she felt. There's something unique about being a student, and sometimes I regret not appreciating it enough at the time. It's easy to get caught up in the moment, to stress about deadlines, worry about what to wear for that big night out, whinge about boring tutors and complain about having to do your own washing.

But all too soon it's over – so make the most of student life. When else are you going to have the chance to live so close to so many friends? Or be able to stay up all night partying or working or simply watching endless films? In the not-too-distant future late nights will become tinged with a daily awareness of a job to go to, or responsibility to face, or an early-morning alarm clock. But as a student you can do whatever you want, whenever you want to do it.

From the time that you fill in your UCAS form, you know that your university degree will stay on your CV forever. But you might not realise that so too will the thousands of memories you'll make at uni. My uni friends and I now spend hours

TIP

'Practise wearing your mortarboard before you graduate. Feeling everyone's eyes bore into you while your weird black hat covers your eyes and makes you fall over when you go to pick up your degree is really not a good way to remember the day...'
Anon, 21, Aston

reminiscing, with whole conversations where every sentence starts 'Do you remember that day…?' before laughing over the time when two of us grew terrified by a caped figure on a walk in the pitch black at 4am, or the day when someone blocked a whole drainage system by putting a massive haggis down the loo as an April Fool. It's taken about a year, but now we even laugh about the frenzied hours spent in the library before dissertation deadline when there was a huge argument about who got to use the industrial stapler first. Really.

Hopefully you'll leave uni will more than just a few extra letters after your name – who knows, you might even know what you want to do with your life! But, either way, on campus you'll gain incredible memories, photos, friends, advice and opportunities. So, enjoy it. Dress up, sleep in, work hard, play harder, meet people, do new things, learn lots.

Wishing you all the best for an amazing student life.

LDT, August 2009

Uni lingo

Sometimes your tutor will say something you can't understand. It might be to do with your course – in which case I can't help. (Unless it's happens on the same topic as my thesis on post-9/11 responses in contemporary American literature.) But if there's some kind of strange-sounding academic or campus term, you might just find its meaning decoded below. Here's a guide to some of the most common 'uni words' and what they mean.

Abstract A couple of paragraphs summarising a dissertation, often required before students submit work that counts towards a degree.

Academic year The university year, normally running from September/ October to June/July.

Access funds Money that universities offer to help students in financial difficulty.

All-nighter Working (or going out) all night.

Alumni A graduate of a university.

Attila (as in the Hun) Slang for a 2.1 degree.

Bachelor (of Arts, Education, Science, etc.) The undergraduate degree you're almost definitely working towards, abbreviated as BA, BSc, BEd, etc.

Balls Big parties, usually involving dressing up in suits or dresses, often to celebrate the end of year or graduation.

Bops Cheesy student disco nights, often themed around fancy dress.

Bursary Cash given to students who fulfil particular criteria.

BUSA The British Universities Sports Association.

Campus The area of buildings and grounds that make up a university. Sometimes unis have a few campuses.

Chaplain Person who offers religious support. Usually universities have chaplains for various religions.

Come up/go down Arriving at uni at the start of term (even if you live north of campus), and leaving at the end. Mainly Oxbridge terms.

Credits Points you need to 'collect' (through coursework, exams, attendance at lectures, etc.) to earn a degree.

College A further education institution, or one of the units that makes up the university at a collegiate institution like Oxford, Cambridge and Durham.

Convocation Posh word for graduation.

Department A body in charge of teaching and research in a particular subject. Also known as faculties and schools.

Desmond As in Tutu: Cockney rhyming slang for a 2.2 degree.

Dissertation A long essay that's usually submitted to be marked as part of your degree.

Dons Lecturers, professors, tutors and generally clever people who teach and research at unis.

Entz That's 'entertainment' – student-run events like bops, pub quizzes and karaoke.

Exec The individual person or organising group of people in charge of a particular society or union.

Finals Your third (or fourth) year exams that usually make up a big chunk of your degree. The ill-looking people working towards Finals are 'Finalists'.

First The highest degree classification.

Flunk To drop out of uni.

Formal A posh dinner, usually three courses served by waitresses and waiters, where students dress up in posh togs or even black tie.

Fresher A first year student.

Geoff As in Hurst, slang for a First.

Go down See 'come up/go down'.

Graduand A student who has finished Finals but hasn't yet attended their graduation ceremony (or been awarded their degree).

Graduate What you're aiming at – someone who has completed a degree.

Graduate student Someone with an undergraduate degree who's studying towards another one (also known as a postgraduate/postgrad).

Graduation The ceremony where you wear the world's silliest hat (the mortarboard, that one with the swinging tassel) and are awarded your degree.

Hack An over-keen student journalist or politician who is always trying to get you to sign up for something.

Halls of residence University accommodation blocks.

Jobshop A student job agency, usually based at the Students' Union.

Joint honours A degree like 'Law and French' that includes more than one subject.

Junior Common Room The undergraduate Students' Union at individual colleges (usually Oxbridge) or in halls of residence.

Lecture A formal, academic talk given by a subject specialist to a group of students.

LGBT Lesbian, Gay, Bisexual and Transgender.

Major/minor honours A degree where a student studies two subjects, but concentrates on one (the major subject), while studying a second subject in less detail (the minor subject).

Matriculation At Oxbridge, the ceremony where you formally become a member of the university.

Mature students Over 21s who are studying undergraduate degrees.

Means-tested The way that local authorities decide how much money to give students, dependent on their parents' income.

Module A unit of study focusing on an area. Several modules make up a degree.

Moral tutors See 'Personal tutors'.

Nightline A telephone support line operating at night at most universities, run by students for students to offer help during the night.

NUS The National Union of Students – the body that provides support and services to those university unions that pay to be affiliated, and represents students in areas like the national press.

Oxbridge The group name for Oxford and Cambridge, the UK's oldest universities.

Personal tutors Most universities assign tutors to a group of students, who can contact them for pastoral help.

Plagiarism Copying someone else's work without acknowledgement, to pretend it's your own. Regarded as cheating and usually strongly punished.

Professor Someone at the top of their subject who you probably don't want to contradict too often.

Rag Student charity which raises money through sponsored events like hitch-hikes.

Russell Group A band of elite UK universities, including places like Oxford, Cambridge, Bristol and UCL.

Sandwich course A course which includes (usually a year of) vocational work. Also known as a placement year.

Semester A term, usually lasting about ten weeks.

Seminar A larger-scale tutorial, where usually between 10 and 30 students come together with a tutor for discussion rather than lecturing.

SU Students' Union.

Term The academic year is divided into three terms – blocks of study.

Thesis See 'Dissertation'.

Town vs Gown A way of talking about the relationship between a town's locals and the university population, who, once upon a time, wore gowns on a regular basis.

Transcript A written record of the marks achieved throughout a period of study.

Tuition fees Course fees payable to unis to cover the cost of learning.

Tutor A university version of a teacher.

Tutorial (or tute) A teaching session of a small

number of students to discuss essays, experiments, research, etc.

Undergraduate Someone studying for a first degree.

Union Another way of referring to the Students' Union.

Vice Chancellor Contrary to their confusing name, the VC is the head honcho of a university. Chancellors, by contrast, do not usually take an active role in running a university.

Viva An oral exam where students are grilled about their knowledge of a particular topic – usually only at postgrad level, but can be used if a student is 'in between' grades on an essay or exam to decide which degree to award.

Help and resources

General student information

National Union of Students – the body representing students in the UK has information packs on its website.
www.nus.org.uk or 0871 221 8221

Also: NUS Scotland   – 0131 556 6598
            NUS Ireland   – 028 9024 4641
            NUS Wales   – 029 2068 0700

UCAS – information about applying to universities, available courses and institutions.
www.ucas.com or 0871 468 0 468

Funding information

Student Finance England – a Government source of comprehensive information on student finance and funding.
www.direct.gov.uk/studentfinance or 0845 300 5090
(for English students)
www.studentfinanceni.co.uk or 0845 600 0662
(for Northern Irish students)
www.studentfinancewales.co.uk or 0845 602 8845
(for Welsh students)
www.saas.gov.uk or 0845 111 1711 (for Scottish students)
www.ukcisa.org.uk (for international students studying in the UK)
www.direct.gov.uk/en/EducationAndLearning/
UniversityAndHigherEducation/StudentFinance/

StudentsFromOtherEUCountries/index.htm (for students from other EU countries)

Student Support Information Line: phone 0800 731 9133 for free copies of student funding guides.

Student Loans Company – some local boroughs use the SLC to organise their student residents' loans.
www.slc.co.uk or 0870 242 2211

MoneyFacts – compare student bank account options.
www.moneyfacts.co.uk/banking/bestbuys/banking_stud_accounts.aspx

Bursary Map – map of bursary information for students at English universities.
http://bursarymap.direct.gov.uk

NHS student grants – information on bursaries available for health care students.
www.nhsstudentgrants.co.uk

Armed forces student grants – information on bursaries available for those in the armed forces or interested in signing up to the armed forces.
www.armyjobs.mod.uk/education/grants

Student work and jobs information

Gumtree and **Student Gems** – find and advertise your skills to find work.
www.gumtree.com and www.studentgems.com

Tax advice for students from Revenue and Customs.
www.hrmc.gov.uk/students

Other sources of help and advice

SKILL – information to help students who have a disability or learning difficulty.
www.skill.org.uk or 0800 328 5050

Grants for students with disabilities – charity which provides cash (£250–2,500) to help disabled students in higher education.
www.snowdonawardscheme.org.uk/ or 01403 732899

Drugs helpline – the FRANK helpline is free and confidential.
www.talktofrank.com or 0800 776600. Alternatively, try www.drugsline.org or call them on 0808 1 606 606.

Smoking helpline – free advice from the NHS.
http://smokefree.nhs.uk or 0800 022 4332.

Sexual health helpline – free sexual health advice from the NHS.
www.condomessentialwear.com or 0800 567123.

Gay advice helpline – free helpline for young people affected by homophobia. Each – Educational Action Challenging Homophobia – 0808 1000 143 or www.eachaction.org.uk

Depression and suicide helpline – 24/7 help for students (and non-students) who feel very low or depressed.
The Samaritans – 08457 909090 or www.samaritans.org or email jo@samaritans.org

Alcohol helpline – free number to discuss drink-related problems.
Drinkline – 0800 917 8282

Student discount vouchers

www.studentbeans.com – a huge student discount site with vouchers for meals, travel, entertainment and more.

Student freebies galore with regularly updated free offers. www.studentfreestuff.com – freebies from Sim cards and food to cinema tickets and make-up.

Budgeting tool – helps you to make a student budget. www.studentcalculator.org.uk.

Food and recipe websites

Student recipe sites – find thousands of quick and cheap recipes written for students, by students. www.studentrecipes.com and www.studentcook.co.uk

Cheap-food finder – helps you find the cheapest supermarket for your trolley full of food. www.mysupermarket.co.uk

Shopping

For technology...

Microsoft – www.microsoft.com/uk/student/default.mspx – find out about Microsoft student technology and discounts.

Apple – http://store.apple.com/uk/browse/home/education_ routing/ – Apple's student deals on iPods and iMacs.

For a phone...

www.Onecompare.com – use this site to hunt down the best-value mobile phone deals.

www.skype.com – download Skype to make free calls to friends with the software plus cheap calls to UK and foreign phones.

For books and magazines...

www.bookbrain.co.uk – searches the web to find the cheapest-priced available books.

www.abebooks.co.uk – lists second-hand books around the UK that you can cheaply order by post.

www.student-subscription-service.co.uk – cheap magazine subscriptions including *Time*, *New Scientist*, *Vogue* and *The Economist*.

Your student accommodation

University halls – check your halls are accredited by one of these bodies.
www.universitiesuk.ac.uk/acop or call 0207 419 4111 or
www.anuk.org/largecode or call 0113 205 3404

Find student accommodation – fully searchable list of student accommodation options around the UK.
www.accommodationforstudents.com

Utility bills – get your bills lower by using price-comparison sites. www.CompareTheMarket.com and www.uSwitch.com both compare the cost of utility bills and insurance (including student possession insurance).

Free furniture and more – short of a bed or table in your house? If you're lucky, you could grab one for free on this site, where people list things that they don't want, so you can scoop them up for free.
www.uk.freecycle.org

Travel

National Rail – information on train journeys, destinations and ticket prices in the UK.
www.nationalrail.co.uk or 0845 748 4950

Discounted bus travel – student bus discounts on campuses including Manchester and York.
www.firstgroup.com/students/

Student Railcard – buy a rail card for £26 for discounts of up to a third on national rail services.
www.16-25railcard.co.uk/

Cheap coach travel – www.megabus.com

Student Coach Discount – buy a 16to26 coach card for £10 and receive up to 30% discount on coach travel.
http://www.nationalexpress.com/coach/offers/students.cfm?CFID=28574829&CFTOKEN=16651669

Student holidays – a travel agent just for students, for holidays, flights and all your travelling needs in the UK and abroad.
www.statravel.co.uk

Travel abroad

Study abroad – information on the European Erasmus scheme
www.britishcouncil.org/erasmus or 029 2039 7405 or email erasmus@britishcouncil.org

Erasmus student network – www.esn.org or
00 32 225 67427 or email secretariat@esn.org

Information compiled by Edinburgh University on country-specific websites for students studying abroad.

www.international.ed.ac.uk/exchanges/Erasmus/ERASMUS_
websites.html

Health and personal safety

Emergencies – Police/Ambulance/Fire
Call 999 or, for non-emergencies, contact your local police
station.

NHS Direct – a helpline for medical enquiries and help
locating your nearest medical centre.
www.nhsdirect.nhs.uk/ or 0845 4647

NHS Sexual Health Helpline – available 24 hours.
0800 567123

Personal safety advice – www.suzylamplugh.org/tips

Academic websites

See Chapter 6, 'Work'.

After uni...

Postgraduate funding options – a massive resource on
postgrad funding boards, charities, bursaries and loans.
http://careersadvice.direct.gov.uk/helpandadvice/
helpwithfunding/fundpg/

Graduate jobs – a good resource to start looking for graduate
careers and jobs, plus info on further study too.
www.prospects.ac.uk